T0248100

TIME
IS
NOW

RAJ VERMA

TIME

IS

NOW

A JOURNEY INTO
DEMYSTIFYING AI

Forbes | Books

Published by Forbes Books, Charleston, South Carolina.
An imprint of Advantage Media Group.

Forbes Books is a registered trademark, and the Forbes Books colophon is a trademark of Forbes Media, LLC.

Printed in the United States of America.

10 9 8 7 6 5 4 3 2 1

ISBN: 979-8-88750-203-8 (Hardcover)
ISBN: 979-8-88750-204-5 (eBook)

Library of Congress Control Number: 2024900786

Cover and layout design by Lance Buckley

This custom publication is intended to provide accurate information and the opinions of the author in regard to the subject matter covered. It is sold with the understanding that the publisher, Forbes Books, is not engaged in rendering legal, financial, or professional services of any kind. If legal advice or other expert assistance is required, the reader is advised to seek the services of a competent professional.

Since 1917, Forbes has remained steadfast in its mission to serve as the defining voice of entrepreneurial capitalism. Forbes Books, launched in 2016 through a partnership with Advantage Media, furthers that aim by helping business and thought leaders bring their stories, passion, and knowledge to the forefront in custom books. Opinions expressed by Forbes Books authors are their own. To be considered for publication, please visit **books.Forbes.com**.

To my Kaz

CONTENTS

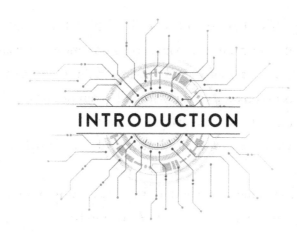

INTRODUCTION

I n 2011, Marc Andreessen famously wrote, "Software is eating the world." He cited the example of Borders, one of the largest brick-and-mortar bookstores, which famously decided to hand over its online business to Amazon.

Amazon is now worth $1.3 *trillion*. Borders, on the other hand, no longer exists.

In the years since Andreessen made this statement, the world has witnessed a litter of companies that have folded under the tsunami of the software wave, often touted as the "Third Industrial Revolution." Blockbuster and Circuit City, to name a few, have become clichéd business school case studies of what *not* to do in the face of fast-moving technological changes. In reality, no company was left untouched.

Then came the pandemic. Not that you need me to remind you, of course.

Vast populations across the world were forced indoors. The lucky ones used the internet and software to stay in business. Every industry had to find innovative ways to conduct business in a zero-touch fashion. The ubiquity of QR codes is a sobering reminder of this trend.

During this phase of the so-called Third Industrial Revolution, not only did more companies consume more software; some companies *turned into* software. Comcast, Hulu, DoorDash, etc. are all now pieces of software we carry around in our pockets. Companies that couldn't adapt just went away.

With AI, we are now dead center of the Fourth Industrial Revolution.

Many companies are poised to become AI driven, or as the last round taught us, they will turn into AI themselves.

Unlike the last round, though, this time it's not merely the adoption of technology that will decide the mortality of businesses. Rather, it is going to be about how companies manage the fuel powering all AI.

Data.

The piles and piles of bits and bytes of information companies have amassed in databases. What many don't realize is that their data defines the identity of the company itself. It's not so different to how we humans are defined by the years of data we collect in the form of our memories. These memories inform our perspectives and differentiate us from each other.

Data is at the core of AI. A company will eventually use its data to make decisions with AI—which will help it form its identity to stand apart from its competitors. Without data, one might think artificial intelligence is just an incredibly fast and powerful computer. But without data, AI is actually of no use to anyone. Once you start feeding it the right data, though, it can amplify human intelligence and performance.

The provenance for the quest for artificial intelligence can be traced to early visionaries who were driven by a singular focus: the ability to synthetically replicate human intelligence. But what is intelligence if not the ability to make choices in Real Time? After all, both humans and companies are the sum total of all the choices they make in Real Time.

And by Real Time I mean what we experience as *Now*.

The Three Pillars of Now

Our environment is constantly feeding us data—information that our brains must then interpret to make the best decision possible. As an avid lover of golf, I can assure you that no golfer who cares about their score swings mindlessly. Instead, they gauge the conditions at the time of the swing—the direction of the wind, the distance to the green, the position of the water trap or sand trap—to decide *how* they will swing. The slightest error in positioning will send the ball astray—and then they have to manage the repercussions.

With AI, we have an opportunity to create new insight on which way the wind is blowing, so to speak. It becomes the caddy with the insight to say, "No, now is the time to use the 3 wood, not the 2. Shift your left foot one inch forward for optimal power."

As the world moves faster and faster, AI will continue to develop exponentially. As it does, the very definition of *Real Time* will change. It's natural for change to accompany a sense of uncertainty. Yet in the long run, we are the ones who reap the benefits when the impossible becomes possible.

Today, none of us think twice about turning on our GPS and following the directions it provides. I've yet to meet the person who wants to go back to carrying a paper map they have to glance at while in traffic. We don't have to be even that drastic. Remember when GPS apps did not have traffic information? Now we take it for granted that the directions change automatically, rerouting us to avoid unexpected traffic or a road closure based on fresh data. This is the power of Real Time.

To keep with the highway analogy, all technology requires a power source, and in the case of generative AI, the fuel is highly curated fresh data. The more fuel in the tank, the farther and faster we can go.

As for the boundaries of the technology highway, who sets them? Who is deciding the speed limit? Who is painting the lane markers?

This is the opportunity and responsibility before us as leaders—to draw the lane markers so we can harness the power of Now to amplify human capabilities while avoiding a collision.

We must consider the long-term impact of the decisions we make. As humans, we have an obligation—a moral responsibility—to think beyond Now. As leaders, we must use this power to not only improve our personal score, if you will, but to improve the entire game. We have to elevate our vision above the narrow focus of Now to consider the far-reaching consequences of our decisions.

Working backward from the moment the decision is made, one could argue that there are three components—or pillars—that come together to form the moment of Now:

Information. A vast collection of moments, transactions, and data has accumulated over the years. This unique corpus of data and the way each data point is connected to another is memory, which serves as the foundation to define your identity. Erase someone's memory, and you take away their true identity. If you have a massive repository of well-connected data, you are considered knowledgeable and even wise.

1. **Context.** Using this memory and vast collection of data, we perform reasoned analysis. These are further nuanced by layers of our own opinions formed by the circumstances and people around us. This context generates emotions, coloring our analysis of the data.

2. **Choice.** Finally, there is the moment we use context on top of memory to make a decision. It is the impetus to create a new moment—the moment of Now.

Life, as we define it, is a series of Now. What will we do with it?

Time Is Now

Before we can decide how to use AI, we have to understand its relation to Real Time. We must first pause to consider the power of Now: How it is shaped through Information, how it is given Context by technology and human behavior, and how it drives Choice. The moment we are in is not isolated—it has been shaped by the past, is powered by the present, and molds the future.

Therefore, this book will be divided into three sections:

Part I: How We Got Here

This section will be semi-autobiographical, showing my own journey and the powerful impact mere seconds—a single decision—can make on one's destiny. My story rides the wave of technological change, in the shift from typewriters to computers, from door-to-door sales to the seismic shift in the world of selling online. Throughout these stories, the technological and cultural seeds were being planted that would lead to generative AI.

Part II: Where We Are

This section will take a look at the reality of today and where many companies find themselves. Again, this will mirror parts of my own story, including my journey into Silicon Valley, leading up to when I became CEO of SingleStore. This is not because I have all the answers but because I myself am on a learning journey as a student of how Real Time, data, and AI are impacting our world.

Part III: Where We Are Going

As generative AI evolves, there are implications and decisions we all must make about how we will shape our future. After all, there are companies utilizing data in such a way that they know more about what you will do next online than you yourself do. On top of this, we must recognize how the changing speed of Real Time and information sharing can be both a competitive advantage—and the spark that lights the powder keg.

The question most are facing now is "What do we do with AI?" Before we can answer this, however, we must demystify AI. We must understand what it should and should not do. While artificial intelligence holds great potential for good, it also wields great potential for harm. So how do we as leaders make decisions that are in the best interest of society versus what is only best for profit?

This last point is the heart and soul of this book. In this era of AI, data, and the acceleration of Real Time, we have a responsibility as leaders to pursue a *conscious* capitalism, where a profitable organization imparts its value to employees, customers, and the community as well. The choices we make bear weight beyond the bottom line and will impact generations to come.

In light of this, we need to become more conscious about *what* we do, *why* we do it, and *how* we do it. We must make a shift from "Can we do it?" to "How are we going to do it?" We have to accept that while we will never reach a state of perfection, we can find meaning and solace in the process of incremental progress.

Perhaps you are reading this and couldn't care less about my personal journey. If so, I take zero offense to it. If that's you, by all means skip ahead to chapter 8, where the conversation shifts to the future and to demystifying artificial intelligence. While part I and part II could be seen as the appetizers and salad, part III is the main course. Although you will miss some of the context from the lessons beforehand, part III can still serve you as a practical guide.

In the end, it's about deciding now what kind of world we will have tomorrow. We can be selfish and afraid—or we can be courageous and selfless. I am optimistic that we can choose the latter.

History has shown us that the present is better than the past. The future can be better than the present if we are good stewards of Now. This is not the time to exploit or run away from the potential of generative AI. Rather, with the right information available to us placed in the right context, *Now* is the time to leave an impact on this world by choosing to do what's right.

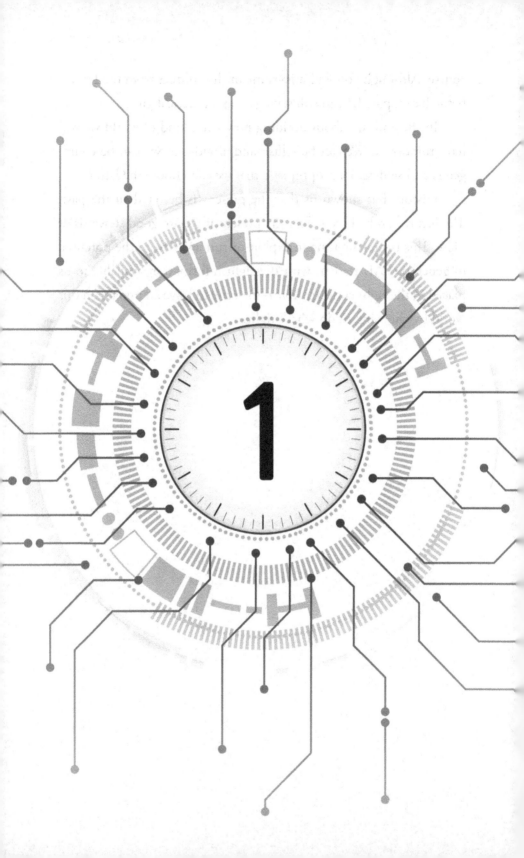

HOW WE GOT HERE

The Power of Now

Every human heart beat is a universe of possibilities.

—GREGORY DAVID ROBERTS, *SHANTARAM*

Life is a series of Now, and each passing moment has echoes of the past and will have reverberations into the future. Our memories are made of the information we take in throughout our lives and give us our identity. The current context gives us impetus. How we choose to act in the Now is what makes us, us.

This book is about my journey of the discovery of Now and how the three pillars of Now—Information, Context, and Choice—helped me shape a billion-dollar company specializing in transacting, analyzing, and contextualizing data in real time to amplify human intelligence and capabilities.

While this book is centered on my story, life has taught me that our stories never belong to us alone. They are part of a greater story begun long before we came into the world—a tapestry of moments woven together from the decisions and choices of our ancestors.

In the rush of life, it's easy to forget the impact a single moment can make. It's easy to neglect the power of Now. Until Now comes rushing toward you to change everything.

On a gorgeous February day in 2010, such a Now met me head on. It had been a mild winter in the Bay Area, and I was into CrossFit at the time. While recovering from my workout, I was feeling pleased with myself and thinking about the day ahead, which I assumed would be filled with chasing around my little ones.

I was still in my workout clothes when my phone rang—and I saw it was my mother calling me from India. Knowing how uncharacteristic it was for her to call at such an hour, my heart skipped a beat. Whatever she had to say, it was unlikely to be good news.

My fears were confirmed right away. My grandmother had passed away. The grandmother who had helped, in a substantive way, to shape me into the person I am today.

My mind rushed back to the last time I had seen her—my cousin's wedding years before in Delhi. After the wedding, my life had been filled with a series of moves from country to country.

Sorrow washed over me mixed with regret. Year after year, I'd told myself, "Next year, I will make the time to go visit." But now? I would never see her again. An extreme river of grief flowed through me, and I so regretted the carelessly discarded yesterdays that I will never get back.

> "Life is a series of Now."

This Now I was experiencing was a combination of three pillars— my memories of my grandmother (Information), my emotional analysis of her loss (Context), and my own decision to delay visiting her despite knowing the limited time I had left with her (Choice).

As the Buddhist thinking goes, "Life is a series of Now."

This is the true power of Real Time. In a single moment, your world can be altered. Knowing how to act in that moment requires great discernment. It necessitates knowing where you have been, knowing where you want to be, and deciding how you want to get there.

The implications here are not only personal—they are interpersonal. They are global, even. Our actions ripple to impact others for generations. Our stories are shaped by events that preceded us. To repeat the opening quote, they open a "universe of possibilities."

To understand the power of Now, we must become students of how it forms through Information, Context, and Choice. By doing so, we can become the leaders the world needs by becoming better humans.

Information

In technical terms, our memory is the collection of the data that shapes our identities. The longer we live, the more information we take in. Yet it also includes the events that happened *outside* of our control, before our lives began.

It wasn't until after my grandmother died that I learned she had been adopted. In life, she had been a strong, self-possessed woman. I adored her for all she was—she filled rooms with her infectious laughter and walked with the grace and dignity of a highly educated person despite the fact that she had no formal education herself.

The circumstances of how she ended up alone at less than a month old, whether she was abandoned or whether her biological parents had died, were never clear to us. The best we can piece together is that she was likely orphaned from a Brahman family in India. When my paternal great-grandfather heard about her circumstances, he made a split-second decision to bring her up as his own daughter.

Part of his motivation in this was likely the circumstances that faced orphaned children in India. It was a very unsafe world for such children, who often ended up begging on the street or being forced into sex slavery.

Meanwhile, my paternal great-grandfather was a merchant of some means. Even though he was newly married at the time, when he caught wind of an orphaned newborn, it stirred his compassion. Within this context, he and his new bride—my great-grandmother—made the choice to adopt my grandmother, their hearts overflowing with a generosity and kindness they passed on to her.

This single decision, now frozen in time, not only changed her fate but created mine. In 1936, at the age of thirteen, she married my grandfather. He was working as a government servant, a clerical worker in the British Empire, trained to be subservient to the Raj, something that seems so far-fetched in the world I inhabited decades later. He put his head down, rode his bicycle to work, and on his way dropped off his kids to a government school in what is now known as Old Delhi.

They lived together in a one-bedroom, government-sanctioned house. As my father told me many times, it was a happy home. "We grew up not knowing want," he said—a sentiment that could not be shared by everyone.

My dad then went on to become an officer in the Indian Army. By the time I was born in 1970, he was doing well for himself and our little family.

As one might expect in a military family, we moved a lot, and at one point he was assigned to a field position in Ladakh on India's border with Tibet and China. Families could not go there, so my mother and I moved to Delhi to be with my grandmother, aunts, and uncles. When I was age three to six, we lived in the same house all together, and I was fortunate to spend so much time with my grandmother.

Every morning at six thirty, I'd wake up eagerly, much to the surprise of most adults in the family and specifically my mother. I loved to accompany my grandmother to the Hindu temple. She would take a brass container, and I would help her collect fresh flowers to submit as an offering. In those walks, I observed her piety and her kindness, and I learned the nature of karma. The serenity of the temple, the sounds, and the basic act of sitting still was very appealing to me. Very peaceful. I surprise myself today as I recollect how I felt at that rather young age.

She taught me, "If you do good, good will come back to you. The universe is not good or bad but reactive."

I found extreme solace and serenity in those experiences with her, and my mind goes back to her lessons often. Even after my dad was reassigned to Kanpur and we joined him there, I would visit her every summer and continue our ritual together. When she came to visit us, she would follow the same routine at the local temple.

As she cultivated my soul, my mind was cultivated at home. Our house was a typical Indian home in that education was always the highest priority. Growing up under British rule, the philosophy of my grandparents was simple: "Your country can be invaded and taken over, drought can take away your crops, but nothing can take away your education."

As a result, almost the entire side of my father's extended family has a master's degree. Since I was an only child, our nuclear family's agenda was centered on my schooling. It was important that I was at school on time, wearing the right uniform, with all the resources I needed to be successful. After school was sports, and my dad's army life afforded me an opportunity to play tennis, squash, and billiards, and during the blistering heat of the summer, a nice cool dip finished off the evening.

In school, there was a huge emphasis on what we would today call STEM, especially the math and science portions. Fortunately, I was good at math, but what really caught my attention were these new things called computers entering the school. We were taught the basics of coding, such as the Fibonacci sequence ... which may sound trivial now but was magic in those days. While I was never set on becoming a developer, I credit those lessons with teaching me the power of structured thought—something I treasure to date.

Having such a template in my mind is the greatest aspect to which I attribute my modest success. The value of structured thought is one I've paid forward to my own children, ensuring they have a basic foundation for programming because of the mental advantages it provides. This is the ethos that has carried forward from my family's value of education—to educate yourself as much as you can because it's never a waste.

From an uneducated, orphaned child, married at an early age to a kind man, who then went on to raise a family, my grandmother is the genesis of my journey. A journey that led her great-granddaughters to be strong, independent women attending some of the most sought-after educational institutes in the world. I think you can tell, I am proud of my daughters. And equally proud of my older son, who too embraced a similar path. With my youngest child, little Chance, who is at the ripe old age of six as I write, I can't be objective, as I truly believe his only role is to be my reason to be deliriously happy! He has in his possession the best golf swing I have seen.

All these events have helped shape me into who I am today. Without the choice my great-grandfather made to adopt my grandmother, my father would have never been born. Nor would I.

You can say the same for yourself. From a genetic standpoint, your Now was decided by a billion other "Nows" that came before. Those

Nows opened doors that would never have opened without them and led to helping you make choices you never thought would present themselves. We often seem to refer to that as luck, but it just may be the reflective nature of the good choices made way before we had a choice. Similarly, the future is being decided with each Now. What you choose matters. Way more than you think. In life and in business.

And much more when you have a never-before-available tool like AI.

Context

When you think of Real Time, what comes into your mind? Maybe it's a phrase like *right now, in a flash, instantaneous,* or *in the blink of an eye.* For me, I think about the world of navigation.

For thousands of years, humans have relied on the stars to gain our bearing in the universe and to help us chart direction across the sea. By knowing the position of the stars and planets at any moment, one could deduce one's position on the earth. But how real is this type of Real Time? Think about that—sailors were making real-time decisions on direction based on light that was millions of years old!

As technology changes how we can accomplish our goals, it changes the definition of *Real Time.* If a ship captain today insisted on using the stars to guide their way when they are equipped with a state-of-the-art navigation system, you'd insist on having a new captain.

Growing up in India, I constantly had to ask people for directions. I was dependent on the knowledge of others to figure out where to go and how to get there. Even if you were traveling by train, you had no say in the path itself. You just consulted the train schedule based on when you needed to arrive at your destination. This was Real Time.

Then websites like MapQuest came along, allowing us to see multiple options to navigate our way. We felt more in control of the journey and could print out the directions immediately rather than having to wait for an updated map to become available. This was also Real Time.

Today's Real Time is the AI-enhanced GPS you rely on to navigate your commute. You can think of Real Time as the blue dot that indicates where you are in the moment. You can see where you just left—and you have some predictive data on what lies ahead. It may tell you where to turn for the fastest route, but you are the one who must turn the wheel.

As the speed of Real Time has increased, so has the level of control we have. We have more power to decide what to do at any moment. These decisions carry great weight, not only for ourselves but for the world around us. With this power, we have a responsibility to ask ourselves *how* we will use it.

Before we can act, then, we must first learn.

It is no different with AI. The heart of AI is data—that is, the information it learns. If we see AI not as *artificial* intelligence but as *amplified* intelligence, it means we must recognize that these tools have the potential to both help and harm. The difference is in who has the control—us.

We control the data. We steer the ship.

Consider how the printing press revolutionized communication. A machine was able to print a Bible in a fraction of the time it took for monks and scribes to do by hand. For the first hundred years, this was the primary use of the printing press. But eventually it would be put to use for other purposes—literature and politics—disseminating information in a way that changed the fabric of society.

We have seen this do much good in the form of literacy and innovation. We have also seen it do much harm in the form of slander and misinformation. The printing press itself does not decide the moral direction of what it prints—we humans do.

For leaders, this should be our daily food for thought: How are we utilizing the tools before us? Are we being responsible? Are we doing good for the world over the long term—or only what is good for ourselves or for the quarterly report?

Real Time thinking is never isolated to the current moment. It looks back, shaped by the data. It gains nuance and color from the context of the present moment. And it uses these to look ahead. It sees the power of Now to influence the future, to drive our choices.

Choice

As a teenager, I admit I had some pent-up resentment for what I viewed as my parents' overrotating on education in their parenting—what some refer to as "tiger parenting." Specifically, I didn't understand why I had to study for six hours a day when I knew I could finish my work satisfactorily in two hours. Why not have four hours for myself to enjoy life?

As a result, when I went off to university, I overrotated on having fun with my newfound independence. Six months in, I realized I had to take accountability for my grades and learned to better ration my time between study and fun. In the end, I was able to strike a balance and graduated in the top 10 percent of my class with a degree in computer science.

To this day, I credit my college experiences with my lifelong love for how technology can shape the world. Yet upon graduation, I had to confront the first major decision of my young adult life.

The world was very different back then. Not everyone getting out of engineering school got a job. I wasn't sure what I would do next—look for a job or stay in school and go for my master's.

One day, some representatives from Wipro came to a campus recruitment event. The company's founder was a rising star who went on to become one of the wealthiest men in the world, though he wasn't there yet at the time. Still, the presence of the company caught my attention as well as the attention of many of my friends.

They offered us the opportunity to take an exam that would then determine if we could move on to the interview stage. Despite my high grades, I failed the exam and wasn't selected for an interview.

In fact, it was so competitive that literally *no one* from my college got into Wipro. This was no comfort to me, though. It was my first taste of failure as an adult, and I hated how it made me feel. When I told my dad about failing the exam, his response was "Welcome to the real world. You'll always have a home here if you need it."

He meant this to motivate me, but I took it as a rebuke. I committed to myself that no matter what I had to do, I would not resort to moving back in with my parents. I would leave no stone unturned.

As I discussed my options with my friends, they said, "Raj, we haven't ever met a more convincing guy than you. You should go knock on the door of Wipro headquarters and ask for an interview. If anyone can do it, it's you."

I was a little shocked by the suggestion. After all, was it likely Wipro would offer me an interview when I had just failed their test? What if they just kicked me out of the building? Still, I had nothing to lose. I agreed I would give it a go.

At the time, I only possessed one pair of professional-looking pants, and my friends helped me iron my one collared shirt in preparation. Just to be clear, I am not romanticizing my limited means—I had plenty of fashionable clothing, just nothing I could wear to a professional interview. I walked into the first floor of the Wipro headquarters and said, "I'd like to see HR—here's my résumé."

Instead of chucking me out as I had expected, the woman considered me, took the résumé, and asked me to sit down. I sat there for only a few moments when suddenly the head of HR came out and invited me into his office for an interview. Ninety minutes later, he asked me, "Raj, what would you like to do? Sales or technical?"

I didn't know what to say. After all, I had shown up on a total whim, egged on by my own determination and some positive peer pressure. And now the head of HR was offering me a job? I decided to defer to his expertise and asked, "Where do you think I would be better suited?"

He felt I would do best in a go-to-market role and said, "Come back next Monday."

My heart sank. "I can't," I apologized. "I'm actually headed to Bombay."

Then he wrote a message and a name on my résumé and handed it back to me. "Give this to *that* person at the Wipro office in Bombay." I wondered if I had just passed up a one-in-a-million opportunity, but I had made a promise to be in Bombay, and I needed to stay true to my word.

Following through on my commitment, I caught the train to Bombay, where a friend drove me to the Wipro office there for another shot at an interview. I repeated the same exact routine as before: I walked in, asked to speak to HR, and handed over my résumé. After another interview, I was offered my dream job.

It was my grandmother's lessons on karma returning to me. I had taken a chance on something good, and now something good had come to me. Now I had the responsibility to do something with the opportunity I was handed.

Whether it was a whim or destiny, my choice to walk into Wipro changed the direction of my life forever. I found myself taking the leap from student to professional, living in Bombay, the financial center of India at the time, with its bright city lights.

This momentary decision had led to my first break. Looking back, I see this was another instance of Real Time making an impact in my life. I've taken many chances in my life, but there have been five big ones that have shaped me, this being the first. In doing so, I learned one of the most valuable lessons in my life: you're not going to score on the chances you don't take.

> You're not going to score on
> the chances you don't take.

Soul and Mind

Whether you are a spiritual individual or not, approaching Now ethically requires a cultivation of your soul and mind. In making any decision, we have an ethical responsibility to consider the outcomes— the consequences of our choices. The mind behind the choice must be in balance with the soul of the choice.

For example, consider the algorithms built for social media platforms like Facebook and Instagram. The end goal has often been to keep people on the platform, since increased engagement leads to more ad sales, more revenue.

With this business-first goal in mind, a group was given an assignment: "What does the ideal teenage girl look like?" This was a demographic they wanted more engagement from, and soon enough, a profile of the "ideal teenage girl" was developed by an algorithm. In turn, the "ideal teenage girl" algorithm promoted certain content, knowing the engagement would go up.

While they achieved the end result of more engagement from their target demographic, they also peddled anxiety, as teenage girls were bombarded with images and videos of what their "ideal" appearance *should* be—according to the algorithm, that is. As you can imagine, this can result in all manner of mental health issues for teen girls, from questioning their self-worth, to exhibiting eating disorders—issues which I will touch on more later.

Now, certainly Mark Zuckerberg didn't know about this exact profile being developed. He didn't specifically order a profile that would create mental health issues for teen girls. This was not the intention. But nonetheless, the choices made at the top of Meta about increasing engagement and revenue through algorithms, with no forethought to the consequences, still demand accountability.

As a dad of girls myself, I'm deeply concerned about these issues, which has prompted me to read a lot about them.[1] I care about how my daughters see themselves and want them to be confident in who they are. I want them to cherish the values my grandmother taught me—kindness, respect, decency—over notions of physical appearance.

This is what I mean by cultivating one's soul and mind. If Meta had considered the societal impact of creating an "ideal teenage girl" profile, they could have altered how they went about it. Just because we have the knowledge to take an action does not mean the action will be of benefit to the world.

With generative AI—or any other emergent technology—we must be cautious in our approach for how we use it to further our agendas. Whether it will be used for personal or professional purposes, we should look at ourselves as whistleblowers. We need to be asking, "What's the ultimate goal of this project? Is it going to bring good into the world?" These are questions that should be asked in a public forum to gain insight, not hidden away in a locked boardroom.

---

1   Greg Lukianoff and Jonathan Haidt, *The Coddling of the American Mind: How Good Intentions and Bad Ideas Are Setting Up a Generation for Failure* (New York: Penguin Press, 2018).

When we can combine Information and Context through this lens, we can make better Choices, not only for ourselves but for the world and for the future.

A Full Set of Clubs

I love golf, but I didn't grow up playing it. Instead, I was first introduced to it by two American politicians—John F. Kennedy and his brother Robert.

During summers in college, I would go back home to Kanpur. I didn't have many friends who still lived there, so it could be a little boring. One day, I found myself watching a documentary on a black-and-white TV that featured JFK and RFK playing golf together.

I was immediately fascinated. I had to try it for myself.

Because of his military status, my dad had access to a local golf club yet had never been there himself. I went to him and declared, "Dad, I want to learn to play golf."

Though he had never played it either, I suppose he saw my request as a good excuse to spend time together. He went out and borrowed a set of clubs from a friend and got some caddies, and we went to the club to play. I can still remember taking my first swing with a 9 iron on a course next to the Ganges River. To this day, I don't know how I managed it, but I ended up hitting it well. That was all it took for me to get hooked and begin my love affair with golf.

Beyond the game itself, it's about the experience for me. I love the smell of the grass, the early morning dew, and the social aspect. Three months after my first swing, both of my parents and I were golfing together every day, making great memories. I learned then that you can know a person for years and not know their true character until you play a round of golf with them.

Part of the beauty of the sport is what it does for my mind. When you play golf, you're not actually playing against another person. You're playing against *yourself*. When you have a club in your hands and the ball in front of you, you can block out everything else. It's extremely liberating.

As in life, you can't control every detail in golf. You can't control if an unexpected gust of wind comes along right as you swing and carries your ball into the rough. But you *can* control how you adjust.

Once more, this is the power of Now, the possibility of responding in real time. When your ball goes off course, you can adapt and choose the club you know will get you back onto the fairway. And while no golfer ever intends to end up in a sand trap, you'd better have your sand wedge ready just in case.

As we approach how to handle decision-making in this book, think about what you have in your proverbial golf bag. Are you carrying only drivers? If so, you won't be able to finesse your second shot on a par 5 hole. If you're carrying only a putter, you're not going to get very far at all. You need a full set of clubs, equipped for whatever situation comes up.

Having the right tools at your disposal is what can empower you to take the right swing for the right situation. Looking back, I can see now that the influence of my grandmother, the focus on education from my parents, and my own self-drive gave me the clubs I needed to navigate the transition from childhood to student and from student to professional.

Generative artificial intelligence tools are just another golf club to use. It's a matter of using the right club for the right situation—a combination of Information, Context, and Choice. In golf, problems arise if you carelessly grab a club and swing without considering the conditions around you—the wind, the location of the sand trap, your foot position. The same is true with AI.

No one is perfect. You're not going to hit a hole in one every time you take a swing. Nor do you need to. You just need to keep swinging—not blindly, but using the skills you've acquired to select the right club for your next swing. Celebrate the birdie when you get it, because you'll need it to offset the time you're stuck with a bogey.

While I had no influence over my grandmother's adoption any more than I do the wind blowing across the golf course, I still use her powerful influence to help me adjust my swing in life. She may be gone, but her teachings will always be with me to help me know how to wield each Now I've been given.

There will be many detractors in life trying to take you off course—family circumstances, competitors, or even your own mistakes. The gift of Now is having the ability to learn from your setbacks (Information) and gain the necessary perspective (Context) so you can improve your swing (Choice). This is the power of Now.

The best part is, we don't have to settle for letting the future happen *to* us; we can instead take part in how it happens. We have been facing the highs and lows of technological advancement for thirty years now—the challenges before us are *not* insurmountable.

Instead of defining AI as "artificial intelligence," what if we thought of it as "amplified intelligence"? When used correctly, it has the transformative power to make our lives better, to amplify the good in us. After all, it is our free agency—Choice—that sets us apart from AI.

One of my favorite Steve Jobs quotes is when he said, "When we invented the personal computer, we created a new kind of bicycle … a new man-machine partnership." On the surface, this sounds backward. Why compare your invention to the bicycle? Why not a car? Digging deeper, the analogy is brilliant.

For one, there is the speed factor. In terms of speed in the natural world, we humans are average at best. But put us on a bicycle? We can go faster than most animals—and farther. For another, there is the agility factor. A car may be faster than a bike, but it has fewer options available to it. It must stick to the road. A bike is more agile and can go over terrain and through passages impassable for an automobile.

With generative AI, we have a new bicycle. It can make us faster and more agile, changing the definition of Real Time. But like for a bicycle, we must be the ones to pedal it in the right direction.

In the combination of Information, Context, and Choice, through the lens of soul and mind, we can find the right direction—and the right moment and time. The question remains: Are we brave enough to do so?

Practice Makes Relevant

There are no mistakes. Only new paths to explore.

—GREGORY DAVID ROBERTS, *SHANTARAM*

It would still be years after college before I became conscious of Real Time as a concept. Yet part of the power of Now is that it is always at work, whether you recognize it or not. The key is your actions and attitude.

We often define luck as being "in the right place at the right time." We attribute it to happenstance. But these are the questions we should be asking: "What do I need to do to find the right place? What can I do now to leverage the right time when it happens?"

The headline-making developments in AI may feel like they just dropped out of the sky, but these changes have been long in the works. One has only to look back at the events of the past thirty years to observe the shift in how technology and business have been woven together. One can see clearly how the drive to "work smarter, not harder" has paved the way for where we are today.

Where some companies seem to get lucky compared to others, there is much more to the story. If you know the full story, you will see actions they took in the background to become successful—these actions led to their "luck." The "lucky ones" have been practicing for a *long* time—learning from success and failure along the way. Successful individuals and companies exert discipline, even in the course of innovation. They do not allow discomfort to derail them from the end goal.

As I stated earlier, Real Time is never just about the present moment—it's always about looking ahead. While AI has many applications, prediction is one of the most important for organizations. But before we can consider how the combination of AI and Real Time is leading us into the future, we need to take a moment to look back at its infancy.

While we could probably go all the way back to ancient history and examine how our ancestors created the first tools to become more efficient, this would be overkill. Instead, let's go back to thirty years ago, when computers still felt like props from science fiction movies, not everyday staples of the common office.

Learning Curve

If the story of how I got the job at Wipro wasn't audacious enough, the sense of ambition I felt on my first day definitely was. I can still pinpoint standing outside the headquarters, feeling the breeze, and soaking in the scenery, an overwhelming sense of purpose coming over me in the moment. I made a promise to myself there—to make a name for myself, yes, but to also be the best version of myself.

The ambition of this promise to myself is especially notable when you consider I had literally no idea what I was going to do walking in on day one. My new title was "marketing executive," but I had no further information about what this would entail. Nor was there any hint of how I was about to become part of the technological revolution that has shaped our world into what it is today.

So there I was, twenty-one years old, dressed up for my first day, when a man walked up to me who has since become a dear friend. He said, "You are new here, right? Marketing executive?"

"Yes," I replied.

He gestured for me to come over to the window and pointed to a set of buildings rising from the cityscape. "You see that group of buildings there? That's called Nehru Place," he explained. "You see the tallest building? That's not your territory. See the next-tallest building? That's not your territory ..."

He continued like this for another minute, pointing out the buildings that were "not my territory," before finishing with "The remaining nineteen buildings—*that's* your territory."

Still clueless, I asked, "What do you mean by territory? What am I supposed to do?"

He answered, "You go up to a building at nine thirty every morning, take the elevator to the top floor. Then take the staircase back down, knocking on every office along the way to see if they want to buy a computer or printer from us."

Yes—I was going to be as literal a definition of door-to-door salesman as you could ask for. And this is exactly what I did. On the days when there were no power shutdowns, I would take the elevator to the top of a building in my territory. Otherwise, I took the stairs. I then knocked on literally every door, starting at the top, saying, "Hello, I'm from Wipro. I sell PCs."

Half of the people who answered would tell me, "Leave a card. We'll contact you." Naturally, none of these ever contacted me. The other half were curious and asked, "What do you do?" And we would have a conversation in which I would explain about computers. After all, the idea of an office computer was still very new at the time, so many people had no information available outside of our interaction.

As most salespeople have experienced, there were also the standard rebukes for being a salesman. One of my colleagues shared with me early on, "Look, we are in the business of selling, so keep your ego out of it. It's not personal. You're there to sell."

This became one of the great lessons throughout my professional career. It's allowed me to not take the occasional insults personally but to remain focused on my goals.

So I would do this for hours, day after day—take the elevator up, lugging equipment around with me, and knock on doors all the way down. Then at five o'clock, sweaty and exhausted, I'd head back to the Wipro office to finish out the day.

We had a gentleman manning the office phone who was more or less the receptionist/typist and would answer anytime someone called in to ask about our computers. One of the smartest moves I made early on was to befriend him. Eventually, our friendship emboldened me to ask him, "If you get a lead who calls in, would you mind handing it off to me so I can follow up on it?"

My first sale ever was an Epson printer sold for 10,000 rupees, which today would be about $1,500. I was ecstatic I had sold *something* after so much diligent effort, taking the elevator up to the top floor and working my way down, building after building.

Selling Relevancy

Pretty soon, I figured out that the greatest selling point was the idea of *relevancy*. This was the context I had to create for people. I had to show prospects the problem they didn't yet see: becoming *irrelevant*. The business landscape was shifting, and I had to show how computers would keep them relevant.

Automation—one of the biggest buzzwords in the AI landscape—is no more than how you create relevancy. For example, at Wipro I learned how to pitch prospects not on every feature of the computer but rather to zero in on one aspect that would make their office more efficient, more relevant. Often, this meant explaining the power of word processing to them.

At the time, businesspeople would use a Dictaphone or dictate messages to a secretary who would then type out everything. But there might be mistakes that needed to be fixed or a new thought to add in, meaning the message would have to be retyped.

"You can make changes more effectively now," I would say. "And as soon as you're happy with it, you can print it out, ready to go. Or if you have a fax card on your computer, you can fax it directly from your computer to the recipient."

While I had no concept of Real Time yet, it was the reality of what we were doing—leading prospects down a path that moved their operations closer to Real Time. The way I thought of it at the time was that we were helping people modernize the way they worked. We were increasing their productivity factor—which I found incredibly fun and invigorating.

> I found I wasn't just selling a machine.
> I was selling relevancy.

I found I wasn't just selling a machine. I was selling relevancy. The closer you are to Real Time, the more relevant you are. In doing so, I was also selling defiance of the status quo. I was selling *change*. Anytime I managed to get a prospect to change the way they had been working for the past thirty years, I found it deeply fulfilling.

In short, I became addicted to selling. Honestly, I probably made more mistakes than everyone else put together—but that means I also learned more from making those mistakes. I got better at selling *because* of my mistakes, which got me promoted faster than my peers.

Thinking back to my first day, I was a blank slate with no idea where I wanted to be. But through sales, I found where I *needed* to be—on the cutting edge of what technology could offer to the world.

Considering the tools available now, I can't help but think how much easier my job would have been if I'd had today's AI capabilities back then. Instead of manually going door to door in an office building, what if I could have fed an AI model with the data about everyone in the office building—their job title, their company's products, and so on?

Instead of spending hours going up elevators and down stairs, a program could have told me, "Here are the twenty offices you need to target today." No question that this would have given me a leg up on the competition.

Or what if instead of having to ask my friend for a lead, the prospects' inbound lead information was automated to be given to the salesperson with the greatest chance of success? Obviously, this was impossible back then—the tools didn't exist. The computer age had only just begun.

But for those of us in the present, we have to consider this carefully. What tools are available today that can make us more competitive, more productive, and more efficient than we were yesterday?

This is where AI-first thinking must enter into a leader's mind. What process can be automated? What system can be made more efficient? It's not about replacing people with technology. It's about empowering people with technology for impact.

This is the context of relevancy at work. If you seek only to exploit AI for momentary selfish gain, you do not have a relevancy mindset. Remaining relevant always looks *forward* and *around*. It asks, "How will this impact the next generation? Will this do good or harm for my fellow human?"

Discipline and Freedom

In time, a new opportunity arose—software. The choice was between continuing to sell hardware only or explore this new area of software.

To many at the time, selling software felt like a fool's errand. To clarify, you must remember that this was a time where hardware and software were indistinguishable. Also, you have to understand the cultural context that intellectual property was unknown in India at the time. Some rightfully asked, "Who's going to pay 100,000 rupees for a disc?" On the surface, it was ridiculous. Many of my colleagues at the time chose to stay in hardware because it appeared to be the safer route.

As I look back, this thinking seems foolish on their part. But in the moment, their skepticism appeared logical with the available information in the given context. Hardware was at least tangible—software was intangible.

Selling software meant moving upstream. A societal shift still had to occur. Common objections were statements such as "Why should I pay millions of dollars to access this information? Why not do it myself? What if it doesn't work for me?"

Remember, I had already made a choice to live on the cutting edge of tech. At Wipro, I discovered how much I loved the "aha moment"—that transformational moment of optimism and enthusiasm when prospects realized there was a better way to do their work.

When I was approached by PTC to sell software, they were offering me sixteen times the salary I was making at Wipro, so I said to myself, "Look, I'll give it a shot, and if it doesn't work, I can go back to hardware."

In software, I saw the chance to try something new, to find a new avenue to bring people their "aha moment." Without a ton of case studies and proof to point to, I acquired the ability to be creative and paint a picture of the end result. I had to learn the problems in order to figure out the solutions.

Specifically, PTC's software was focused on automating the manufacturing process with computer-aided design software. Back then, if you designed a product, you would make a mechanical drawing, then a mold would be made, and then the mold would go to manufacture the product. However, let's say you discovered you needed to tweak the design. You would have to go all the way back to a new design on paper, make a new mold, and so on. It was time and resource consuming.

With software, though, you could design the product on the screen—and if you changed one dimension, the other dimensions would automatically update the designs and drawings down the line, saving time and money. It felt like literal magic when we demonstrated it to manufacturers.

At first, I didn't know exactly how to sell software, but I felt if I applied the skills that had helped me sell computers and printers, I would stand a good chance of success.

Contrary to popular belief, discipline gives you freedom. Just like at Wipro, I learned to show up ready to learn every day. It took me a good four to five months to really understand the software enough to start being successful, but I remained disciplined. When you are disciplined in your approach, it frees you from all other thoughts that might pull you off the path of success. It frees you from ego, from pride, from self-pity. It keeps you focused on the end goal.

By 1997, when I was twenty-six, I had become the highest PTC seller in India. At this point, PTC selected me for one of their boot camps, where they would fly in the most successful reps to demonstrate their product knowledge. More than any kind of personal development, these boot camps were about identifying the best of the best. You had to know everything about the product, inside and out. If you failed, they would fly you back home—the end. It was like *The Hunger Games* of software selling.

Going in, I didn't know what to expect. Wanting to ensure I performed well, I prepared more than anyone else at the boot camp. One of the leaders at the boot camp was Brian Halligan, who would later go on to become CEO of HubSpot. He wanted to use the boot camp to select a top sales rep to become the new director of sales enablement for the entire region.

At the end of the training, I was held back by the instructor Kelly Land. He asked me, "How do you think you did?"

Not wanting to appear overly confident, I returned the question, saying, "I'm not sure. How do *you* think I did?"

He said, "I think you did exceptionally well."

Turns out, he was right. I had put in the work, prepared well, and the coveted position of director of sales enablement became mine. Yet this meant I would have to move to Hong Kong from India, thousands of miles away from anyone I knew.

I was blown away. I couldn't believe what was happening. As excited as I was about the opportunity—and the substantial increase in salary—there was also a nagging feeling within me saying, "But why should you leave India? You're comfortable here. You know what you're doing. You're already making good money, and you're happy.

What if something goes wrong? How can your family help you if you're so far away?" All these thoughts were valid. But they were the wrong thoughts for remaining relevant.

If you allow it, comfort will hold you back from progress. Freedom is in discipline, yes, but it is also found in the willingness to face discomfort.

Software had given me wings, so I had to wonder, *What else can technology do? Where else could it take me?* Little did I know then how impactful my choice would be. No one in the world could have predicted the seismic shift technology would make across all sectors in the coming years.

So I accepted the position—and left India for Hong Kong, where I would be thrown into a new position, a new culture, and a new way of thinking about the world.

Afterward, the narrative that formed was "Raj got lucky." I don't blame anyone for thinking this, but it's simply not true—at least, not in the way they meant it. The truth is, I found that the more I practiced my craft, the luckier I got. This is true in all aspects of life.

> The more I practiced my craft, the luckier I got.

I *chose* to be more disciplined than everyone else. I learned everything I could about our products, leveraging the love of learning my family had instilled in me. Instead of going out drinking the night before work, I chose to get plenty of rest so I could show up well the next day. It was about finding pride in my performance, pride in making a difference.

Remaining Relevant

In this age of generative AI and the ever-shifting definition of Real Time, the risk of becoming irrelevant is greater than ever before. To overcome the risk, there are some misunderstandings with the current tech climate we as leaders must confront.

For starters, there is a notion in the market that to embrace AI, you must throw caution to the wind. While it is true that innovation always requires a level of risk taking, a brave willingness to face the unknown, this doesn't mean you have to ditch order.

On the contrary, this is where discipline sets you free as you change. Both at Wipro and PTC, I had no clue at first how to sell the products I was responsible for. I was at the forefront of an industry shift. Not only did I have to sell a product, I had to sell the vision behind the product—I had to sell the innovation.

I could never have done this without the discipline of knocking door to door, of dedicating myself to show up every day and give my all. It's not innovation to throw out all rules of conduct—that's anarchy. Unfortunately, we have too many companies in a rush to modernize that are throwing darts to "see what sticks," but they have no target, no dart board.

Discipline gives you the dart board. It gives you a place to aim.

I had no idea back then that I was riding the wave of technological and industrial change. The concept of Real Time still eluded me, and yet looking back I can see how the discipline I had learned in my youth and through sales equipped me to stay above water while riding the wave.

The other misunderstanding is that discomfort should be avoided. There will always be a temptation to remain comfortable, especially when things appear to be going well. I could have remained in India and lived a comfortable life on my salary. But I would have missed out on the growth that only comes through discomfort.

Even when you are disciplined with your approach to modernization and tech implementation, there will always be some discomfort.

The gut reaction is to flee from it, to go back to "what works," to what is comfortable. Selling software was not a natural transition for me from selling hardware. It was months before I gained any traction. Yet it was in the discomfort, coupled with my discipline, where I found success.

One of the most valuable lessons any successful person must learn is to get out of your comfort zone. Going to Hong Kong was a *massive* step out of my comfort zone. I had to focus on the bigger prize ahead—the joy of progress. Despite the uncertainty involved, I'd already promised myself to stretch my God-given abilities and seize the opportunities afforded to me by circumstance. I could not go back on the promise now.

To this day, I get a dopamine rush every morning by asking myself, "How can I stay on the cutting edge?" To put it another way, "How can I remain relevant?"

To use a golf analogy, if you only practice putting a foot away from the hole, you will never improve. But if you practice from eight to ten feet away, at a scale of discomfort to get out of your comfort zone, then maybe you will get better at putting. Even then, is it still possible to have an off day on the golf course? Yes. Life is never perfect no matter how much you practice. There will always be factors out of your control. But practice teaches you how to better adapt to those factors.

The secret to success is not how hard you work nor how much you know. It's what you do consistently, and it's how relevant you are. I have had colleagues who were brilliant yet never challenged themselves and stayed at status quo, fixating on incremental improvements. In time, they became irrelevant.

Is hard work important? Yes. Is knowledge important? Yes. But they are ingredients. Practice not only makes perfect; it makes you more *relevant*.

Not every AI tool will work for you and your company. It takes practice to find which ones work. When I golf, I favor some clubs over others. I have only discovered this through practice.

Becoming irrelevant happens faster now more than ever—for both individuals and organizations. You only remain relevant through sustained effort. You can "go viral" and be forgotten in the same week. Practicing with discipline through discomfort makes the difference in staying relevant.

> Practicing with discipline through discomfort makes the difference in staying relevant.

As a final thought here, practice keeps you on pace. The pace of technology seems hectic right now, but this is only because we have forgotten how hectic life felt twenty years ago. We tend to look at the past with rose-colored glasses and forget the detail in the experiences we had, only focusing by comparison on what is happening now.

Yes, AI is disruptive. But so was the shift from typewriters to computers. So was the shift from hardware to software. So was the shift from brick-and-mortar selling to e-commerce. But if you are always practicing—applying discipline in the face of discomfort— you can keep on pace, remaining relevant no matter what the next change brings.

Low Chance of Success

In the end, everything will be okay.
If it's not okay, it's not yet the end.

—FERNANDO SABINO, *THE CHECKERBOARD*
(TRANSLATED FROM PORTUGUESE)

The fear of risk is natural. Call it your inner voice, your gut, your intuition—when we detect risk that makes us uncomfortable, we turn the other way. We choose the path that appears safest.

Is this not how banks choose whom to lend to? They assess risk and approve those loans that are the least risky, denying the ones that are more risky.

In the corporate world, it is no wonder leaders have been conditioned to be risk averse. Risk is seen as the enemy of success. The unfortunate consequence of this belief, however, is assuming that anything new is *too* risky. Under this view, leaders default to the status quo. Stagnation occurs and, eventually, decay.

Life is inherently filled with risk, though. The new is inherently risky because it does not yet have a track record of safety behind it. There is always an element of the unknown.

Where some view AI as too risky, too new to embrace, I'd like to offer up an alternate view. What if artificial intelligence, in bringing us closer to Real Time through its analysis of highly curated data, can actually help us *reduce* risk? What if it can improve our predictions about which course is worth pursuing?

> Many of the AI tools emerging now are designed for this purpose—to help us see what we cannot see on our own. To help us reduce risk and find the smarter route.

Appearances can be deceiving, after all. Remember the scene in the animated film *Finding Nemo* when the two fish—Marlin and Dory—approach the dark, foreboding trench? Dory had been forewarned that swimming through the trench was safer than swimming over it. Marlin, who was not privy to this knowledge, has only appearances to work from. Afraid of what he sees, he insists they swim over. This lands them in the midst of a mass of deadly jellyfish—which could have been avoided if they had acted on what was *not* obvious.

Likewise, many of the AI tools emerging now are designed for this purpose—to help us see what we cannot see on our own. To help us reduce risk and find the smarter route.

What looks safe can end up being treacherous. What looks risky can end up being the innovation of the century. How many of us wish we could go back and invest in Apple at its inception? Or Microsoft? Or any of the game changers from the past forty years, for that matter?

First things first: you must accept that you can never avoid all risk. The question is this: How do you increase your chances of success when the odds are stacked against you?

A common theme throughout my life has been taking opportunities that appeared to have a low chance of success. This began with walking up to the Wipro office and asking for an interview when I had already failed their assessment exam at my college. This was also true in my decision to shift to software sales just as hardware sales were booming.

It's also been true in my personal life. Just ask my wife.

Creating a Second Chance

If there is one action you can take to guarantee happiness in life, it's to pick your life partner well.

I was smitten the first time I saw Karen in high school. I immediately began to ask around about "the new girl," on the hunt for any information about her. Unfortunately, it wasn't love at first sight for her. When I finally asked her out, she turned me down. Not long after, I went off to college and lost touch with her.

Until I moved to Hong Kong in 1998.

Globalization as we know it today was picking up speed. With the rise of the internet, the world became both bigger and smaller all at once. In the difficult decision to leave India, I found myself exposed to new ideas, new cultures, and new people at a rapid rate—a buffet of the world, if you will.

I had become friends with a flight attendant from Amsterdam, and one day she said, "You know what? I just flew with a new flight attendant on my crew—she's so pretty—this girl Karen who's also from Bangalore."

"Karen Jones?" I exclaimed, my heart leaping.

My friend was amazed I had gotten this right—what she didn't understand was how exotic a name *Karen Jones* is in a large Indian city like Bangalore.

All of a sudden, I wondered if globalization was about to bring me another chance with my teenage crush. All I said aloud, though, was "Wow, I'd love to get in touch with her."

Eventually, I was able to wrangle Karen's phone number and called her up. When she answered the phone, I said, "You probably don't know who I am, but I'm an old acquaintance from Bangalore."

"Don't tell me who you are," she said. Before we had been on the phone thirty-five seconds, she guessed correctly it was me—to my surprise *and* delight. Better yet, she was willing to meet up with me while she was in Hong Kong.

I know this will date me a bit, but I had a PalmPilot at the time. When we met up, I asked if she would mind holding on to it, so she slipped it into her purse.

Unfortunately, this was the high point of the date. Very quickly, I could see how nothing I said appeared to be of interest to her. I was making no impact, and my attempts to salvage the date failed one after another.

Finally, it was time to throw in the towel and call it a night. Mostly on her part, because I probably would have kept trying to make an impression as long as it took. We said an awkward farewell and parted ways. Within five steps, a thought struck me: *My PalmPilot. It's still in her purse.*

The most obvious action to take would have been for me to turn around and say, "Sorry, I need my PalmPilot back." After all, she was still close enough to easily make this happen. But I knew if I did this, I would never see her again. Meanwhile, if I let her hold on to it, then I would have an excuse to see her. At least once more. I could create *another* second chance.

LOW CHANCE OF SUCCESS | 47

When she eventually found the PalmPilot, she called to let me know. I tried to make this an excuse for another date. But she made it clear in no uncertain terms she was *not* interested. I thought to myself, *Fine, it's done. I blew it.*

Then she said, "I'm flying to Bombay in a couple of days, and I'm having dinner with someone—you can come by and pick it up there."

When she said "having dinner with someone," I knew what she meant. She was going on a date with another man, not just a friend. And now I would have to be in the awkward position of asking for my PalmPilot back in front of her new romantic prospect.

It only got worse as I walked up. I could see them through the window of Dan Ryan's there in Hong Kong. Objectively speaking, her date was an incredibly good-looking guy, and they were facing each other at an intimate table with a lit candle between them. I can only imagine what I looked like as I slunk up to them and muttered a pathetic, "Hi." She had seen me coming and already had the PalmPilot extended to keep our interaction as short as possible, a clear indication to make myself scarce.

Then opportunity knocked in the form of her dinner partner. To this day, I don't know what his motivation was for what happened next. Perhaps I looked so sad that he felt sorry for me, or perhaps he had a twisted sense of competition. Whatever the case, he invited me to join them—to Karen's surprise but my delight.

I immediately took him up on the offer, pulled up a seat, and joined them. I took the opportunity that had somehow fallen into my lap, even as improbable as the outcome may have seemed to most. Having the courage to fight for something you love was about to be out on display.

My driving motivation here was all about spending a little more time with her, since I knew this could very well be the last time I ever saw her. I am sure most will agree that high school crushes are special—they seldom become reality. So having an opportunity to spend an evening in her company was something I could not pass up. The fact that another guy was there was a minor detail.

Over some interesting cocktails and some appetizers, we all talked. My sense of humor was spurred on by every incremental cocktail. We laughed and spoke fondly of our common friends—including her little sister, who had been with us in school. We talked about how life in Bangalore was so different from life in Hong Kong.

Candidly, it was an authentic, genuine conversation between two humans with a common past. We were completing each other's sentences, and I could not help but notice how beautiful she looked and how her laughter lit up the room (it still does) and how much she loved potato skins. For those hours, I was just a boy who was talking to this girl he had harbored a crush on for a decade.

As they say, when you want time to slow down, it only goes faster. Hours had flown by, and eventually she had to go home, as she had an early flight to Bombay. We walked her to her taxi, and I gave her a hug, knowing it could be the last. Even so, it felt good to have spent that evening with her, and I just hoped she felt the same way.

After waving goodbye, I skipped my way to the nearest bar, an ear-to-ear grin on my face the rest of the night. When I got home, I had a voicemail from Karen saying, "I'd love to see you again when I get back from Bombay." We did, and fortunately for me, I have been waking up next to my high school crush—now sweetheart—ever since.

We all have our own unique love story—mine was this Anglo-Indian girl who'd had possession of my heart since I was sixteen. We moved in together, and every day was a pajama party. We talked, we laughed, and we planned what the future may be for us. All of that in a seven-hundred-square-foot apartment in Lam Tin. Navigating the world together from that tiny apartment remains one of the happiest times of my life.

To this day, I recognize how globalization helped bring us together. Largely thanks to technological advancement, globalization brought me an opportunity I never could have imagined. While it's possible our paths could have crossed again in India, globalization increased the chances significantly.

Without giving too much away, globalization would also help open the next great opportunity in my career. Today's generative tools—especially artificial intelligence—have opened up to us a global wellspring of knowledge previously out of reach. The wise person never assumes their context contains all necessary knowledge but rather seeks out knowledge.

The rest is history. Our life together has not been without obstacles, but as they say, love conquers all. We got married in two separate ceremonies. In fact, the first time I ever set foot in a Catholic church was for my own wedding, which was then followed by an Indian ceremony. We danced, tasted every dish, and made sure we enjoyed the day to the fullest. And so we embarked on the most exciting journey of our lives—marriage. At times, it felt like it was just the two of us in a small dinghy, in the small hours of the night, going down the rapids without navigation. It was unknown, and at times frightening, but always exhilarating!

Together, we moved from Hong Kong to Australia and then to California in 2006. To this day, Karen remains the love of my life, and we have built a wonderful life together with four beautiful children—more to her credit than mine, of course.

None of what I have experienced in life, with all its highs and trappings of success, would have amounted to anything if Karen wasn't in my life.

When it came to a low chance of success, this time around I *did* get lucky!

Embracing the New

In the face of increasing globalization, we leaders have an opportunity to increase our chances of success—especially in light of how AI can assist us in creating new insights. We have the rare opportunity to look at what is happening across the world, find the greatest ideas, and embrace them.

During my time at Parametric (PTC), the environment could be described as a stereotypical intense corporate culture. There was a warlike mentality—a cutthroat internal competition driven by a mindset of extreme performance management and extreme account-ability. Yet to this day I'm grateful for how my time there opened me up to so many new ideas that have served me well over my career.

With the insight of age and experience, I can look back and see where I've had to unlearn some of the "performance at all costs" mentality I picked up, but this is part of personal adaptation. As you develop, you learn new and better ways to work. What made you successful years ago does not equate to making you successful *now*.

But at the time, given my own personal values of discipline and embracing discomfort, there were aspects of the dog-eat-dog corporate culture that brought out the best in my work ethic. As such, this period of my career was marked by experiencing anything new and novel that came my way. I was a young buck, ready for adventure. Having left behind the familiarity of my homeland, I embraced the *unfamiliar*.

If a new opportunity arose, my instinct was to jump on it. I was committed to the cutting edge. This can be a dangerous place, yes—but I was addicted to the excitement it brought.

As you've likely picked up from the last chapter, being faced with something I've never done before has never fazed me. Instead, I find the intellectual challenge highly motivating. I like to dive in headfirst—sometimes before I know the depth of the water.

Anyone in a sales-based role knows how much singular dedication it requires to succeed. As one colleague pointed out to me, it seemed like there was a law of attrition. That is, if you just stuck with it and dedicated yourself to staying around, others would fall away from the burnout and you would be left to rise up the ranks.

PTC was still new in the Asia-Pacific landscape, so opportunities to stretch myself and learn new skills were abundant. In time, I left Hong Kong behind, living in Singapore, New Zealand, and Australia.

It was during this time that I first became aware of the power of Real Time by hailing a cab on my mobile phone for the first time. The year was 1999. It was mind altering. At that time, I was living in what I consider to be one of the cleanest and most phenomenal countries in the world—Singapore. For those of you who don't know Singapore, it is located on the equator, so it experiences the same climate every day, sunrise and sunset are at the same time, and the temperature can be summed up in one word: *hot*. If I didn't finish my run in the cooler air before seven, I'd be sweating all day. And just like clockwork, at four in the afternoon, a rain shower occurs.

I liked the rhythms of the city, and I planned my day around them, including the taxi ride to and from work each day. One of my colleagues noticed that I would stand by the curb at the end of the day and wait, hoping I could grab one of the taxis driving by.

One day, he said to me, "Raj, let me show you magic." He took out his mobile phone to book a cab, punched in some numbers, and told me his cab was on the way. I thought he was crazy. Lo and behold, he took my phone, showed me how to do it, and both of our taxis showed up. It was amazing.

Once you have something that makes your life so easy, you come to expect it. We get used to these amenities in life, and I got used to hailing a cab via my mobile phone. But then I would travel to Sydney or Mumbai, and they hadn't yet caught up. But it would just be a matter of time.

Even then, AI was creeping up on us. While I didn't see the direct connection yet between software and Real Time, I was keenly aware of how the advent of the internet and early mobile computing was going to fundamentally change the world and upend the status quo for all of us.

Dismantling Status Quo Culture

Here is another misunderstanding we must correct as leaders: innovation is not technology. Innovation is about culture. It's about facilitating a culture in which it's okay to challenge the status quo, to try the new.

I say this because we see the same pattern within every technological change. The companies who resist ultimately die. And when they die, they are unable to see that their death started ten, twenty, maybe even thirty years before.

Less than fifty companies have been on the Fortune 500 list every year from 1955 to 2022.[2] If you zero in even further, you'll discover that over half the Fortune 500 companies from the year 2000 are now nonexistent.[3]

Throughout my career, I've begun to see a simple variable between successful and unsuccessful people. It's not talent or brains. It's the willingness of someone to challenge the status quo and try something new and difficult, even if it means failing.

Always shoot for perfection. Settle for excellence.

---

2   Tristan Bove, "These 49 Companies Have Been on the Fortune 500 Every Year since 1955. Here's Who They Are," Fortune. com, May 24, 2022, https://fortune.com/2022/05/24/ fortune-500-companies-list-every-year-exxonmobil-chevron-pfizer/.

3   Ryan Berman, "Business Apocalypse: Fifty-Two Percent of Fortune 500 Companies from the Year 2000 Are Extinct," RyanBerman.com, accessed June 8, 2023, https:// ryanberman.com/glossary/business-apocalypse/.

People and companies who become immensely successful are those who challenge the status quo to the point of irritation. From the outside, it looks like insanity—and most people avoid insanity. But on the inside, it means fresh, new ideas are generated as bright minds ask, "What if?"

Some companies are more suited to embrace an innovative culture. It has little to do with what technology they are using. It has everything to do with the desire to remain relevant.

If you go back to 2004, the ideas behind companies like Tesla and SpaceX sound like the premise of science fiction. What starts out as science fiction eventually becomes reality. Look at the moon landing, the internet, and now the rise of AI. Staying relevant equates to having a growth mindset, one in which you thrive on challenge and see failure as an opportunity to learn and grow. What you knew yesterday does not determine your success today. This is a fundamental tenet of the tech industry.

Yet the vast majority of people are a reflection of what they knew yesterday. The irony here is how often change-resistant companies know too much to go into the unknown. They have unknowingly cultivated a fear of discovery, forgetting the *joy* of discovery.

Globalization is fertile ground for developing an innovative culture. It combines new ideas like ingredients in a dish. You may go through a few batches before you find the right recipe, but once you do, the results are delicious.

Whether you have an innovative culture or not is determined by how people make decisions when the CEO or senior executives are *not* in the room. The journey to relevance—or irrelevance—begins with how decisions are made. Until you can become almost maniacal about practicing and promoting a culture of innovative decision-making, you will never be able to innovate in action.

This is where AI comes in. AI has great potential to cut through the noise that clutters decision-making, find the patterns for us, and more accurately predict the decision primed for success. It cracks open the door of the unknown a little wider so we can better glimpse what's on the other side. It amplifies our collective human intelligence so we can get an idea of what's just around the corner—so we can decide in Real Time.

Let's go back for a moment to my first date with Karen. What if I'd had a heads-up on what topics she enjoyed discussing the most? Or knowledge on what specific qualities she admired the most in a romantic partner? How would this have shifted my chances of success? This would have completely altered my choices during the date because I would have had more context and information. I could have better highlighted the authentic pieces of my identity that were most relevant to her values.

In essence, this is exactly what retailers are doing with your social media data. They buy the data, use AI to identify your patterns about what you value, and then make their decisions on how to provide the value identified. Instead of throwing darts without a target, they now have a target. Not only that—they have a way to make the bull's-eye larger, increasing their chances of success.

Increasing your low chances of success requires great curiosity. It drives you to ask the deep questions that produce deep answers. Curiosity has gained a bad reputation, but in reality, curiosity is essential to dismantling a status quo culture. A curious culture asks, "What can we do better? What can we learn from our mistakes? What are we not doing that we should start doing? What should we stop doing because it's now ineffective?"

Curiosity is the question. Innovation is the answer. Artificial intelligence is simply another tool to guide your curiosity to the answer with the greatest chance of success right now. As we head into part II, you must remember this piece. Because your data—what you know and how quickly you can access the information—has incredible consequences for what you do.

WHERE
WE
ARE

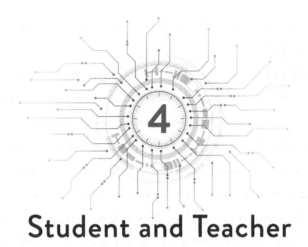

Student and Teacher

When the student is ready, the teacher will appear.

—TAO TE CHING

From the time I walked with my grandmother to the temple to my becoming the CEO of SingleStore, life has always taught me to be a student. You never know where a lesson will come from, what shape it will take, or who your teacher will be. What you can control, though, is having a mind receptive to learning at every moment.

Consider what would happen if your GPS used only historical data. That is, what if it only told you the best route based on what was true last Monday? Perhaps a road has closed since then. Or a wreck has occurred, blocking the way. Instead, GPS couples historical data—what it has learned in the past—with what is happening *now* to determine the best route.

This is a fundamental aspect of Now. While you can certainly learn from the past, never forget to learn from the *present*. Too often, individuals and companies fall into complacency because they are stuck in what they learned from the past, missing the lessons of today.

Perhaps today's teacher will come in the form of a business leader you admire. Perhaps they will come in the form of the airport shoe shiner. For me, it's been both—and anyone in between.

In the early days of my career, and especially while at Staffware and then TIBCO, I was always traveling. I could get a call at a moment's notice, and an hour later I'd be on my way to another country. I was constantly on the move between Hong Kong, Singapore, Mumbai, Sydney, and New Zealand. Sometimes it was hard to keep track of where I was.

One such morning, I received a call from one of our resellers in New Zealand, so I quickly packed and headed to the airport. Whenever time allowed before a flight, I always liked going to the shoeshine station, and this day was no exception.

I sat down in the stall, and the shoe shiner gave me a warm smile as he got to work. Watching him, I noticed that he seemed happy, but I thought to myself, *How can he possibly be happy doing this job?* I had not learned yet that we tend to project our own feelings onto others. I assumed that because I myself would not enjoy shining shoes, it must be impossible for anyone else to do so.

Due to this thinking, I was simultaneously sorry and grateful to be on the receiving end of the shoeshine. But as we struck up a conversation, I made a compelling discovery by listening to the shoe shiner.

He shared that he felt grateful for the chance to shine shoes, that it brought him joy and meaning. "When I'm shining shoes, I think about how I'm helping you succeed today," he said. "Maybe it gives you some confidence, helps you to have a better meeting. If so, that means I got to play a small part in your success."

This, I learned, was the reason for his smile. He poured the joy of this thought into every interaction.

I walked away from the shoeshine station that day with not only a brighter pair of shoes but also a brighter outlook, a sense of inspiration. The shoe shiner I had initially seen as "lower" than me had become my teacher. He had inspired me to be better—to consider how I might enhance someone else's success with each interaction.

This lesson has stayed with me to this day. I've evolved to see my work not in terms of my job title but as the medium through which I could help others become more successful in what they do. Neither life nor business is static. Both continue to evolve, which means I must evolve, too. Learning is evolution. It is becoming aware of the day's lesson to see how you can constantly grow and improve.

There is a mutual value exchange in any teacher-student relationship. To learn, the student needs the teacher. To make an impact, the teacher needs the student. This is a timeless truth that transcends culture.

> There is a mutual value exchange in any teacher-student relationship.

It is similar in our relationship with AI. Artificial intelligence tools rely on humans as the teacher. We must provide it with the data to learn. And yet the result is that AI can then become our teacher and help us learn how to make a greater impact.

Meeting Mr. Real Time

In 2001, I prompted my own change, as I felt my time was up at PTC. There was only so much of that culture I could take, and I wanted to be someplace smaller, somewhere I could make a difference. My next job was with a UK-based company, Staffware, a provider of BPM technology, which was something I took to very easily.

I moved back to Hong Kong from Sydney and was successful in expanding Staffware's presence in the region. Karen and I had just bought our first house in Discovery Bay in Hong Kong, together with our first two kids, living the lifestyle that only Hong Kong can afford. Life was good. It seemed like everything I had hoped my life would be had come true. However, something told me there was yet more to do.

A few years later, Staffware would be acquired by Silicon Valley software start-up TIBCO, the company that became my home for the greater part of my career. TIBCO was founded in 1997 by Vivek Ranadivé, who had graduated from MIT and earned his MBA at Harvard. As such, he was seen as a sort of celebrity for those of us with Indian heritage—the pinnacle of achievement in technology.

TIBCO had enjoyed a huge IPO, so I had read about him before the acquisition and his positive notoriety. I'd be remiss not to mention him, especially as he came up with the term *Real Time*, earning himself the nickname "Mr. Real Time." In essence, he proposed that if you could get the right information to the right person or place at the right time, then you could solve any problem in the world.

Since he was at the forefront of the Real Time conversation, I inhaled his teachings from his first book published in 1999. While technology has changed a lot since then, the philosophies he espoused have not. Without his knowing it, he had become a major influence and teacher for me.

It's no understatement to say that TIBCO, with its philosophy of Real Time, had revolutionized the world of finance. Thirty years ago, if you wanted to know a stock price, you usually had to wait until the next day when the newspaper came in. Even then, you could only see the opening and closing value to determine if you wanted to make a trade. This was the nearest you could get to real-time stock prices unless you went out and bought a stock ticker. Even then, there was a considerable delay between what was happening on the stock exchange and the ticker's information.

Under Vivek's leadership, TIBCO changed this with stock price automation. Now we don't think twice about opening an app on a smartphone to check the value of any stock. Because the data is coming in closer to Real Time, we're able to make more educated judgments on what to buy and sell—and *when* to buy and sell. They had changed the game completely.

On top of this, TIBCO offered enterprise application integration (EAI), and Staffware was integrating people-to-people and people-to-applications. The combined value proposition meant people-to-people, people-to-applications, and applications-to-applications, thereby offering a differentiated value proposition to the market.

My days were filled with evangelizing the value proposition in the Asia-Pacific, and I experienced tremendous success in the region. Little did I realize that this would eventually have a very positive impact on my future and change the trajectory of my life. However, at that time, it was fun, and it was satisfying to see people experience the "aha moment" when they saw how this technology made them relevant.

After the acquisition, I was working with a leading bank in Asia. As the deal progressed, the managing director of the bank expressed a desire to meet with Vivek, someone he had had dealings with in his previous life.

As I sent the request to Vivek's office, I learned he would be in Paris at that time, chairing a company event, and would be glad to host the customer there. The customer agreed, and a few weeks later, we landed in Paris.

With all the flight delays, we barely made it to the hotel before it was time to attend the company event, held at the famous Louvre Museum, a place I had never been before. Like a scene out of a movie,

I found myself at the Louvre in a room with the customer, Vivek, and his young daughter for a private viewing of the *Mona Lisa*. At that time, I recollect I was equally in awe of sharing the room with Vivek as I was with the *Mona Lisa*.

I remember looking around, thinking, *Is this actually happening to me right now? Is this real life?*

The chances of Vivek and me being in the same room at this stage of my career were slim to none. Yet here, opportunity had arisen. An opportunity to learn. Little did I know at that time, like the bridge in the *Mona Lisa*, that I was standing on my own bridge that would take me to an unknown land.

Having exchanged hushed pleasantries in the room with us, Vivek went on to chair the event. I excitedly walked the corridors of the Louvre, putting together the pieces of *The Da Vinci Code*, which I must confess was very joyous.

The next day, the scheduled meeting with Vivek went well, and the meeting ended with the customer feeling reassured of our value, resulting in the possibility for large future transactions.

As the excitement of Paris, the fulfillment of a good meeting, and good old jet lag descended on me simultaneously, I decided to go for a walk and clear my head. There is something about taking in a legendary city for the first time that is difficult to capture in words. As I strolled around the streets, the city's charm and elegance enveloped me like a warm embrace. It is hard—impossible, even—not to feel inspired and hopeful when you see the iconic Eiffel Tower standing tall in the distance, the smell of freshly baked bread engulfing your senses, and the sounds of laughter from small cafés pouring into the alleys, igniting your imagination.

I had seen countless depictions and descriptions of Paris, and now I was finally here. I had experienced the magic of the Louvre, the enigma of the *Mona Lisa*, the allure of this enchanting city, and was embracing an altogether new experience.

Paris, with all its charm and allure, had captured my heart and filled me with a sense of hope and inspiration that I would carry with me long after I left its enchanting streets. ·

Later that evening, while standing at the hotel concierge, I spotted Vivek outside. The customer and I were on our way to dinner and, though it seemed preposterous, I thought, *I should invite Vivek to join us.*

I walked up to him and said, "If you don't have plans, I'd love for you to join us for dinner."

To my surprise, he said, "I'm going to dinner myself right now. Why don't you both join me instead?"

As far as I knew, an invite from Vivek like this *never* happened! I was walking on air as I accepted his offer. For brevity, I won't recall every detail of the night, but I felt like he locked onto me during dinner. He showed a curiosity in who I was, what I did, and my thoughts on the industry.

With dinner concluded, he surprised me yet again when he asked, "Raj, would you like to walk with me back to the hotel?"

Of course I accepted. I would spend any available moment I could to soak in knowledge from this man whom I viewed as a teacher. Yet once again, during our walk to the hotel, he appeared more interested in me. He wanted to hear my thoughts about the advancements in our industry and the role of TIBCO in bringing Real Time to our customers. He was especially interested in my experience related to BPM (business process management). BPM was the driving force for TIBCO's acquisition of Staffware, yet TIBCO's sales team in the US was struggling to sell it.

When we reached the hotel, he looked over and said, "You should come to Palo Alto."

"And do what?" I asked.

"Share your thoughts with the team," he answered. Within days, he emailed to formally invite me to fly to Palo Alto and give a presentation on selling BPM.

Excited, I prepared for the presentation like my life depended on it. I wanted to go beyond discussing the theory of selling BPM and show empirical evidence for *how* to sell it successfully. This was my opportunity to be relevant to TIBCO not only in Asia but in the US.

One of the aspects I planned to include in the presentation was the sales thought process in Asia and how it could be contextualized for the US market. As I mentioned in the last chapter, this is how globalization creates innovation. If you become a student of others who have different life experiences, different upbringings and cultures, you can learn new ways to make an impact. You can take learnings from one context and apply them to another. Some adaptation will be necessary, but this also drives innovation.

It was my first time back in the US in five years, and I'd never been to the Bay Area before. After landing, I rented a car, but I was rusty behind the wheel, as it had been years since I'd last driven myself. It took about seven minutes for muscle memory to kick in and remind me that I didn't need to use *both* feet on the pedals!

The company put me up in the Four Seasons Hotel, and after a good night's rest, I was ready to meet the day. Confident of the work I'd put in for the presentation, I felt it went swimmingly well.

I was initially disappointed when Vivek was nowhere to be seen, but afterward I saw him on crutches and learned he was recovering from a knee operation. He had heard about the presentation, though, and shared with me that the team seemed excited by what they had learned.

I went back home to Hong Kong, where Karen and our two kids were waiting for me. As I unpacked my bags, I told her everything about the trip and the excitement of Silicon Valley. Suddenly, the phone rang. When I answered, Vivek was on the other end of the line and asked, "When can you move?"

Two weeks later, I was in the US as Karen stayed behind to pack up the house. The angel that she is, she never once complained. She and the kids joined me a few weeks later, and we began our adventure in a new country where dreams become reality!

A New Cultural Landscape

On the surface, the decision to leave the Asian market for the US may sound like it was an easy choice. But I promise you it wasn't. In accepting the corporate position, I was actually accepting a one-third reduction in what I had been making. My sales role in Hong Kong had been a commission-paying position, and I was in the top 1 percent of earners in technology at the time. With a wife and two children, I would have been justified in turning down the role.

What made the difference for me was a question I asked myself: *Do I want to be a big fish in a small pond and play it safe, or do I want to take a risk, be uncomfortable, and explore my full potential?*

As great as our life was in Hong Kong, I couldn't pull away from the opportunity to learn in the US. There is no greater place to be a student of technology than Silicon Valley. If I were to continue to learn Real Time, I had to be in the right classroom. As a student, I had gone as far as I could in Asia.

While Karen was very supportive of the move, I admit the transition was fast and confusing and demanded a lot from her. After all, she didn't know how to drive yet, so we had to pick a place to live within walking distance for both groceries and our children's school. Eventually, she did get her driver's license, and we eased into a new routine.

But in the beginning, it was a difficult season. We had to not only learn a new physical landscape but also a new cultural landscape. Even though we had both lived in various countries, the Bay Area was unlike anywhere we had ever been. Not to mention, we also had to help our children adjust to the massive changes while adapting to a different budget than what we had been used to.

Ultimately, the learning opportunity was worth it to me. As I saw it, knowledge held far more value than money. My spirit assured me that everything else would work out.

As a student of Real Time, every day at work filled me with a sense of joy and wonder. I had a voracious appetite to learn everything I could. If I found myself in a group of people complaining about a problem, I'd make an excuse to leave. Then I would surround myself with more ambitious people who wanted to make the world a better place. These were the teachers I chose.

What I have found to be true is that when you are willing to both learn and share what you have learned, you create opportunities for yourself. You give yourself more choices.

On the flip side, when you continue to rely only on previous knowledge, you lock yourself into a box. Your choices become fewer— or else, all choice is taken away as you lose relevance.

Your potential is limited only by how much you're willing to learn and whom you are willing to learn from.

Chasing the Two-Second Advantage

Vivek authored a book titled *The Two-Second Advantage* around the concept that if you can see what is going to happen two seconds before everyone else, you have a natural advantage.[4] This also leads to

---

4   Vivek Ranadive, *The Two-Second Advantage: How We Succeed by Anticipating the Future—Just Enough,* (New York: Crown Business, 2011).

the two-second *disadvantage*—if you're two seconds behind everyone else, you are more likely to fail. This holds true in every aspect of life—relationships, business, sports, you name it.

While the concept is simple enough to grasp, the execution is where it becomes tricky. *How* do you bring about the two-second advantage? This is the seminal challenge of our generation.

But chasing the two-second advantage is also the preemptive nature of today's technology—prediction as we see in learning models and generative AI. ChatGPT is a perfect example here. In terms of marketing, if you can generate a product description and SEO faster than your competitor, then you can go to market faster, generate web traffic faster, and get more sales.

Everyone wants the two-second advantage, but more often than not they experience a form of paralysis when confronted with the changes required of them. They become overwhelmed by the amount of information available, unsure where to begin.

After all, the key to gaining the two-second advantage is in the data itself. I often think about the quote from Fred Smith, the founder and chairman of FedEx: "The information about the package is just as important as the package itself."

In some ways, we are now seeing how the information is actually *more* important than the package.

For example, banks used to have standard opening and closing times. No banking activity could take place outside these hours. But as smartphones became staples in society, banks had to think less about these parameters and more about customer preference. *How* does the customer want to bank? *When* does the customer want to bank?

What they have learned is that most customers don't want to have to come into the bank at all. They want to do everything they can online. In response, the more innovative banks have shut down branches to decrease overhead, built smaller banks, and bolstered their mobile experiences. Banking is no longer about the transactions occurring between nine and five Monday through Friday but a never-ending conversation with the customer. Why?

Because that's where the data is—in the customer conversation. Inside the conversation is the information they need to gain the two-second advantage.

In other words, the two-second advantage exists only when knowledge is coupled with Real Time. In the case of AI, we must be both student *and* teacher, allowing it to learn from us while also leveraging it to create insight.

If you adopt the attitude of a perpetual student, you will find learning everywhere. You will find it from the shoe shiner, your peers, your significant other, and your mentor. While I learned much from Vivek, I could not have gotten to where I am today by learning only from him.

After all, he and I are not the same person. Where he is more philosophical, I tend to be more hands on. This means I've had to both learn and unlearn throughout my career. When a strategy no longer works, I have to gain new skills. I would be a terrible religious leader, because I'm not interested in converting people to my way of thinking. Rather, I want to learn from others' perspectives.

One of my favorite examples of finding the two-second advantage is looking at how the casinos in Las Vegas operate. They are avid students of their customers, learning everything they can about anyone who walks through their doors. With today's AI tools, they are able to develop a profile on every customer, leveraging mathematical models to accurately predict how much time (and money) an individual is willing to lose until they decide to walk out.

By pinpointing this threshold moment when someone is about to leave the casino, they can send a messenger to say, "You're the lucky winner of a free meal" or whatever else they want to offer them based on their customer profile. After all, it doesn't truly cost them anything to offer up a free meal, since it's perishable inventory.

But in offering it up, they give the customer a win. They make them feel good and reset the "losing-streak clock" within the individual. Now the person doesn't feel so bad about how much they've lost because at least they got a free meal out of it. This makes them more likely to stay around longer and see what other win they might gain next.

This is the business value of learning about your customers. When enabled by technology, you can track customer behavior in Real Time. You can more accurately pinpoint what they value, when they want the value, and how they want to receive the value. Infrastructure technology has become an addiction of mine because of how it enables Real Time.

Features like recommendation engines, buying history, and abandoned cart notifications were a few of the ideas keeping me busy at TIBCO. These are now standards in marketing technology that have not only helped businesses chase the two-second advantage but have helped improve the lives of millions by connecting them to solutions faster.

To gain the two-second advantage, though, knowledge must be coupled with creativity. As Albert Einstein said, "The true sign of intelligence is not knowledge but imagination." Some have said my superpower is being able to translate technology into creative application—helping others understand how the technology makes their lives better.

This is where the true monetization of technology comes into play. If no one understands the technology and how it makes their life better, then why would they buy it? Communicating the benefits requires a creative curiosity. It's in creativity that you find the relevancy.

Finally, as I reflect on what I learned from Vivek and how it connects to where I am today, I'd like to borrow a quote from another businessman who lived at the intersection of creativity and technology throughout his career—Walt Disney. He once said, "It's kind of fun to do the impossible."

This idea encapsulates what we do every day at SingleStore, the company I lead as I am writing this book. We work to change the impossible into the possible by learning, leveraging technology to help others improve their lives as they chase the two-second advantage. And you know what? Turns out Walt was right. It *is* fun.

When you open yourself to learn, you create the opportunity to accomplish the impossible.

Creating Insight

We are surrounded by data, but starved for insights.

—JAY BAER

In the discussion about generative AI, much of the focus has been on automation, on outsourcing aspects of human work to become more efficient. This is a limited view, however. The greatest opportunity AI provides for leaders isn't in automation—it's in creating insight. Going from the limited view of what's right in front of you to creating a 360-degree view. The 360-degree view doesn't exist on its own—it must be *built*.

Imagine for a moment you're a pilot. You automate part of your role with the autopilot function—which is really no more than a software program designed to manage the aircraft's systems under certain conditions. It cannot take over tasks requiring human intuition such as the takeoff, landing, or adjusting the route for weather patterns.

Contrast this with the airport control tower. Today's control tower is empowered with AI tools continuously collecting and analyzing all kinds of information—weather patterns, flight routes, aircraft performance—which, in turn, creates insight. Within milliseconds, control tower workers are equipped with vital insight they can pass on to the pilots, who can then make real-time adjustments in their decisions to keep everyone safe.

What happens, though, without the control tower? The best pilot in the world only has a limited view of what is in front of them—even with all their automated systems. They cannot see the trajectory of other planes in the area. They cannot see what conditions are on the ground. Without this vital information, the entire plane is at risk.

You know the expression "there are two sides to every story," but that's not true. There are 360 sides to every story. We have to switch from only worrying about the capabilities of the autopilot—and turn our attention to creating insight from the control tower.

Repercussions

Earlier on, I mentioned the negative effects Instagram had on teen girls' mental health when they developed an "ideal teen girl" algorithm to increase engagement and drive revenue. In 2021, Facebook (pre-Meta name change) admitted they had been aware of this issue since 2019—and had in fact been studying the harmful toll the Instagram app was having on teen girls. These findings have gone on to be referred to as "The Facebook Papers," making headlines around the world.

I have to admit that despite spending my entire career on the cutting edge of technology, I remain mystified by the allure of social media. I only became aware of these reports through a series of conversations with a friend who had teenage daughters at the time the story broke. As a father of four myself—including two girls—I was instantly concerned. Would my kids face the same problems in their teen years? What could I do to protect them from an algorithm completely out of my control?

What struck me was the realization of how differently teens approach social media compared to my generation. For me, it's about sharing special moments and memories with friends and family—and keeping up to date with the special moments and memories of my loved ones. The focal point is on the moment of Now—the memory being created, not the act of sharing.

For teens, however, the act of sharing—and the subsequent response from peers—takes priority. I learned teens were capturing memories for the specific purpose of sharing them in the digital sphere. I found this confusing—they are not living in the moment of *now* because of how much emphasis they put on the likes and comments they want to receive in the future. The dopamine hit comes from the *external response* to an event, not the event itself.

There's a Real Time component for us to consider here. Being Real Time and being *in* Real Time are two sides of the same coin. To put it another way, whom are you maximizing your life for? Yourself? Or to gain the approval of others?

If you take a picture of a sunset because you want to document the joy of the moment, it's healthy to do so. You're experiencing the joy of Now. If you're taking the picture only to gain points through likes and comments, it's unhealthy. When the post doesn't do well and doesn't get the engagement you hoped for, it robs the moment of the joy it *could* have held. The memory is tainted regardless of how splendid it actually was.

I dived into the mental health topic to learn as much as I could, including reading a phenomenal book that I mentioned earlier—*The Coddling of the American Mind*, by Greg Lukianoff and Jonathan Haidt—which has an entire chapter covering the impact of social media on teen girls. I was shocked to hear that the suicide rate among teen girls had shot up ten times in the past ten years, reaching the highest levels in the twelve decades suicide rates have been tracked.

It was sobering, to say the least.

A recent Pew Research study showed that 38 percent of teens reported social media caused them to "feel overwhelmed," and 23 percent said that "what they see on social media makes them feel worse about their own life."[5] As a father, I'm not only concerned about this issue; I've become dedicated to raising awareness around it.

The good news is that emerging tech—including generative AI—can play a role in solving these problems. Take, for example, how the nonprofit Thorn is leveraging AI to expedite the process of finding exploitive images online and identifying where they came from. Since its inception, Thorn has helped identify twenty-five thousand children being exploited online and has become responsible for a large percentage of reports to the National Center for Missing & Exploited Children.

Law enforcement has used Thorn's flagship product Spotlight to accelerate victim identification. It looks for hashes—digital "fingerprints" consistent with exploitive images. This essentially allows them to "look" at images without actually seeing them so they can be reported, removed, and even tracked to the perpetrator who posted the images. In other words, through tagging the relevant data, they create insight on where exploitation is happening and, more importantly, how to stop it.

In addition to this, innovators like Sam Altman at OpenAI appear to be very aware of how their solutions could be misused. Instead of waiting to react to the misuses, though, they are building in safeguards—both to prevent misuse and to increase detection of exploitative use.

5   Emily A. Vogels and Risa Gelles-Watnick, "Teens and Social Media: Key Findings from Pew Research Center Surveys," PewResearch.org, April 24, 2023, https://www.pewresearch.org/short-reads/2023/04/24/teens-and-social-media-key-findings-from-pew-research-center-surveys/.

Likewise, many of the generative AI companies are building in proactive and preemptive safeguards for the problem of sexual abuse and negative mental health effects—whereas social media companies like Meta and YouTube have had to respond retroactively to the damage allegedly done through their platforms.

Which leads us back to social media and the mental health crisis among teens. Whether they are committing suicide because of online bullying, develop an eating disorder because they don't match the so-called ideal, or have fallen victim to online sexploitation, there is a common theme that emerges:

Technology isn't the problem. The problem is how it's being used.

> Technology isn't the problem.
> The problem is how it's being used.

It's a human problem, because we are the ones at the wheel, steering the plane. Without the insight of the control tower, we might not like where we land. We might even crash on the way down.

We can't afford a narrow view of technology's use. We don't get to use the excuse "We designed it for X, so it doesn't matter if it caused Y to happen." We don't have the right to claim ignorance anymore—not when the information necessary for insight is available. Not when we have the tools now for proper analysis. That would be like blaming the autopilot for crashing the plane when the pilot ignored the directions of the control tower.

Instead, conscious and courageous leadership is necessary to protect our children. We cannot ignore the repercussions. The information is available for us to make more ethical, conscientious choices. We have our hand on the controls, so it's imperative we have all the information *before* we land the plane.

Even so, knowing the altitude, speed, and direction is not enough if you do not know *where* you are landing. Context can change everything you *think* you know.

Insight from Trials

No one gets to avoid trials in life. When you are not in control of the circumstances around you, you can either complain about it—or you can create insight from it. One of the most challenging seasons of my career also turned out to help me create the greatest insight into the kind of leader I wanted to be.

Whether you have all the information or not, whether you are in control of a situation or not, context changes everything. It colors the information available. It influences our choices and responses.

During my time at TIBCO, I always felt a great sense of purpose. But this changed when Vivek left. I've always adhered to the idea that when the founder of a company leaves, a part of the ethos and soul of the company leaves too.

Reinventing—or refounding—the soul of a company can be difficult. It takes a rare person to be a refounder like Tim Cook at Apple. In the emotional void of Vivek's departure, I started to look around for new opportunities.

This found me moving over to Hortonworks, but my time there ended after only six months. Though the time was short, I still managed to expand my network and create some insights that have served me well.

Meanwhile, a colleague from TIBCO had gone to work for Apttus and ended up recruiting me to come over and meet the leadership team. I liked the team and the journey they were on—and it spoke volumes to me that the CEO was the founder. From what I could see, it seemed like a great fit for where I was. With this context, I joined as COO.

The first sign of trouble, however, was when my old colleague resigned three weeks later. This surprised me, seeing as this person had played a pivotal role in my coming over.

The real trouble hit in July 2019, when I was blindsided by a report of sexual misconduct involving the CEO and his subsequent termination. Along with my shock, I was devastated. I had hung my professional reputation on the founder—a man I thought I knew. We like to think our reputation is our own, but as I was about to learn, this isn't always true.

In the wake of the scandal, the context of my role completely changed overnight. I was made a part of the CEO office as the board moved to sell the company, including a massive reduction of the workforce so the company could remain viable. No one likes to tell this story. Frankly, I don't like to tell it myself.

Because it was seen as a scandal, it became widely publicized through an article on Business Insider. Unfortunately, this meant a lot of the blowback fell on me due to my close proximity as COO. When the writer of the article reached out to me for comment, I was advised to ignore the request. I complied out of a sense of integrity and loyalty to the company.

In retrospect, I was in a lose-lose situation. Not speaking out seemed to feed into assumptions of guilt. But speaking out would also have been less than ideal. In the years leading up to this situation, the ethos of journalism had changed from the pursuit of a balanced perspective to that of generating clicks—and there was no way to influence such a story primed for clickbait.

As the situation intensified, I even had to hire bodyguards for the office. One day we had a report of a gunman in the building. Even my family's privacy was violated on numerous levels. While I can handle this happening to myself, I hated seeing how my professional context was impacting the people I loved most.

To this day, I don't blame the writer of the article—they were only doing their job, after all. I have no doubt they believed they were doing the right thing by publishing the story. They had no notion of how the article would personally impact my family and others. I feel more certain than ever of my decision to not engage with the negativity. In life, I've found you don't walk away from people to teach them a lesson—you walk away because you've learned yours.

With some time and distance from the situation, I've been able to create insight from this trial. You have to take the good with the bad. The decisions you make can have devastating impacts on people and their ecosystem. There are always repercussions. You won't always have all the information—and you won't always have control over the context in which the information is delivered.

All you can control are the choices you make based on the information you have and the context you find yourself in. Which is why, as leaders, we must make every effort to gain as much information as possible, balanced within the context of Now. When we do, we create the insight necessary to make better choices.

In the age of AI, there is a great lesson to be learned here. Things will not always go your way. Projects will go awry. Mistakes will be made by others that impact you. You must keep in mind that such trials are not the end of the story but a chapter within it. You can always use trials to create insight for yourself on what to do next.

Icarus and the Phoenix

Once the sale of Apttus was finalized, I left. I had gone from the context of great accomplishment at TIBCO to a new context with the back-to-back disappointments of Hortonworks and Apttus.

I felt like I had found myself in the story of Icarus. For years, I had flown higher and higher. Had I flown too near the sun? The jobs

I had taken had been my own choice, after all. No one had forced me into anything.

Every trial presents you with a choice: to be Icarus—or to be a phoenix.

I had learned from both experiences to create new insights. Specifically, my view of what a leader *should* be had grown and evolved. These challenges helped me make the switch from seeing only the view from the cockpit to seeing the view from the control tower.

Two lessons in particular stood out:

First, I had no lack of self-belief in my ability to do more. I still felt I had a lot of music left within me—and I made a choice not to end my career on this note.

Second, I had great clarity that I would never again be a part of anything in which I couldn't have more control of the outcome. With Apttus, I had learned the dangers of hanging my professional future on someone else's reputation. I swore to myself this would never again be the case. Whatever I did next, it would be from my own convictions, not anyone else's.

While I did not know what lay ahead of me, I had never slept so well in my life than I did after leaving Apttus. I had passed through the fire and survived. And I had done so surrounded by my true purpose—not a job, but my family. No matter what happened next, I chose to be grateful.

I made a decision to walk in gratitude the way my grandmother had taught me all those years before. To surround myself with serenity, to believe the storm would pass and that good would prevail.

Insight and Integrity

In writing this book, I wrestled with leaving the unpleasantness in the past. But I realized you can only gain insight if you're willing to look at *everything*—the good and the bad. What would happen if the control tower ignored the approaching storm on the horizon? Lives would be put at risk.

So I became determined that if my experience could help even one leader faced with a difficult situation, then it would be worth telling. If my trials could create insight for others, then it would all be worth it.

Integrity isn't about being perfect—it's about doing what you believe to be right with the information and context available to you. No one can do more.

When "The Facebook Papers" came out, there was documentation and clear empirical evidence of how Instagram's algorithm was proving to be detrimental to mental health. The information was available. But corporations ignored it—not just Facebook, but advertisers, too. As long as content was getting engagement and driving sales, they all turned a blind eye.

In the aftermath, these corporations claimed they didn't know the full extent of the damage being done. There may be some truth to this—but in my opinion, this is only because they didn't care to look at the full picture. They chose only the part of the picture they wanted to see—profits.

The Apttus experience serves as a powerful reminder that while you cannot control the actions or perceptions of others, you *can* control your self-perception. We can learn from both situations, as they highlight different sides of the same issues—insight and integrity.

Insight is knowing the right information in the right context. Integrity is choosing to take moral action based on your insights.

It is this freedom of choice that distinguishes humans from machines. Artificial intelligence can provide us with more insight, more information—but integrity is a choice made within the context you find yourself.

Remember, the secret to success and longevity in business is remaining relevant. To lack integrity and insight is to run into the arms of irrelevancy. If you lose your integrity or lack insight, you will not remain relevant for long. It takes great insight and integrity to see the full picture of the situation—and then make the right choice.

The right choice, of course, is not always so clear. This is the great difficulty for leaders. The right choice can be unpopular. The right choice can be painful. The right choice can go against the best-intended advice. This is another area where artificial intelligence can be leveraged as amplified intelligence—it can help us to predict the possible outcomes and make a more informed, insightful choice. When leveraged from a place of human conscience, it can amplify not only our intelligence but our integrity.

In the next chapter, as we shift to the story of SingleStore, you'll see how these lessons intertwine and combine to shape corporate policy. The information we take in makes our memory, our identity—and this is true for companies as well. Instead of a brain, the information is stored in databases, and the context takes shape through corporate culture. When these meet at the moment of choice, we can embrace the power and potential of Now.

Identity Shift

When a man is interested in the past he writes history;
when he is interested in the future he makes it.

—WILL DURANT, *PHILOSOPHY AND THE SOCIAL PROBLEM*

Comic book superheroes have long been a staple in pop culture, but their stories have often remained on the fringes of society. Yet in the past twenty years, we have seen a shift. Superhero stories are no longer only an interest for children or "comic book nerds" but have entered mainstream culture.

In recent years, films based on superheroes have even been considered for the highest accolades in the industry. They have become regular workplace banter, moments for families to bond over, and the substance for university classroom discussions.

One such example from the Marvel universe is Steve Rogers, who undergoes an extreme identity shift to become Captain America. What's interesting is, he never loses who he is at his core. Under the uniform and muscles, he is *always* Steve Rogers. But in his identity shift, what changes is his ability to influence others by *becoming* Captain America.

Over the course of several movies, he undergoes further changes. Not physically, but in how he sees the world. He is forced to adapt to the modern world and learns he cannot always blindly follow orders. Sometimes protocol has to go out the window and he must make his own decisions based on the context of where he is and what challenge he is facing. Sometimes it means going against the advice his friends have given because he has information they don't have. This requires a different type of courage.

He makes mistakes, too. The key is, he learns from those mistakes. He takes in new information and recontextualizes. This, too, is an identity shift. Great leaders are always willing to make such shifts.

While Steve Rogers/Captain America is confined to the realm of fiction, there is a lot we can learn from his journey:

You cannot change your past, but you can leverage your present to impact the future.

This also is the power of Now. If our past—our memories—make up our identity, then we have an opportunity every moment to shape who we are becoming.

This is true for organizations as well. As I mentioned in the last chapter, we leaders are in the midst of a shift in management. The world is changing rapidly. Culture is changing rapidly. We also must make shifts if we are to retain relevance. This is the great impetus resting within each Now: *Who* will we choose to be?

As you gain fresh information, it goes through the filter of your context. With this insight, it is your moment to make good choices. All three—Information, Context, Choice—are interconnected for us as individuals and as organizations.

For us as leaders, we have to recognize that we cannot shift the identity of others. We have no right to. The workplace and its expectations have changed dramatically since I first started. What was once deemed acceptable has become cancellable. For the most part, the changes have made society better. Perhaps we have overrotated in some aspects, but such overcorrections can be expected in finding the point of balance.

We cannot change the past, but we can influence the future. The Now we find ourselves in gives us the power to do so.

Silver Lining

There is always a silver lining to be found if you look for it. Despite my experiences at Hortonworks and Apttus, what I've learned to be grateful for is how they ripped me out of the status quo.

After my time at Apttus, I knew I needed a shift in identity. Not an overhaul, mind you—but I had been gifted with the opportunity to recuperate, to take some time and not rush into another job but really assess not only what I wanted to do next but who I wanted to be.

Life was treating me pretty well at the time, and as I decompressed, my focus shifted to home life. In particular, I wanted to spend time at home with our youngest son, since I had missed a good chunk of the toddler phase with my other three children.

I also spent a lot of time playing golf, working diligently to become a single handicapper. And when I wasn't spending time at home or on the course, I planned some trips for our family to enjoy the sabbatical with me.

As I mentioned at the end of the last chapter, I looked at how I had gone through two experiences as the "Number Two Guy" in the organization, how I had entered into work cultures that were already well established before my arrival. In every job, you've got to fix stuff, build stuff, and then either scale or operate whatever it is you do. But in these tenures, I now saw that I'd had a disproportionately high component of "fixing" compared to building or operating.

This realization led me to one of my first decisions about how my identity would shift: I wanted to be a builder more than a fixer. Whether this meant I would start something on my own or enter another organization still in its infancy, I didn't know. But my focus would be building.

It was this notion of building that helped me decide I would not be a "Number Two Guy" again. I wanted the opportunity to truly lead and shape a company—to find somewhere I could leave my fingerprints, so to speak. Somewhere I could wield the power of Now to make an impact on the identity of the company itself.

I also took time to consider the nature of my work history. I had always worked within the infrastructure space, with a short stint in the application arena. This had taught me that in the application space, you have a hammer and the world is a set of nails. Every conversation becomes rather convergent—that is, you discuss the same problems over and over again. Whether it is around human resources or financial planning, you encounter the same need and set of problems regardless of who the customer is. It becomes very "plug and play," if you will.

While this is very appealing to many, it wasn't my speed. I gravitated to infrastructure, because there, the conversations were more divergent. That is, every conversation you have with a customer is a new problem, one specific to their identity and purpose.

You can outexecute a poor application. But in infrastructure? Not a chance. Your customers are more informed about their needs than some of your engineers. Your product has to be brilliant to win in this space, because you have to learn; you have to become attuned to who they are and what they need.

Sometimes when you take in new information, it's not only about learning but also unlearning. During this transition period, I spent some time unlearning from my previous experiences. One of the biggest lessons I learned here was that sometimes your strengths can become your greatest weaknesses. With some introspection, I saw how often company founders' weaknesses stem from overused strengths.

One of the founders I had worked with always thought he was the smartest guy in the room. He's not alone—this has been a staple habit among leaders in corporate for a long time. And while he was right much of the time, the one time he was wrong ended up costing the company a major market opportunity. He had labeled an industry shift as a "passing fad," but this then resulted in the company being "late to the club," and they struggled to catch up.

Meanwhile, I've always found more value in the contrarian view—assume you're *not* the smartest guy in the room. Assume instead that brilliance can come from anywhere.

This requires a high level of humility, though. It requires a comfort level with the notion that you don't always need to be the one to have the answers. This was another "unlearning" moment for me in particular. I had to tell myself, *Raj, you do not need to have all the answers*, because this idea had been part of my ethos for so long.

Before I could become a CEO, I set myself a mantra of sorts: "Heart of a servant, mind of a warrior."

This led me to another "unlearning": it is a great strength to change your mind. A long-standing belief in corporate culture is that changing your mind is indicative of uncertainty and weakness. I once believed this myself, but now I wholly disagree with the idea.

When you're presented with new facts, new information, you have a responsibility to take it in and reassess. This has led me to change my mind many times, and I'm now proud of this. I encourage other leaders to do the same.

This is largely what I mean by "mind of a warrior." As Sun Tzu teaches in *The Art of War*, all your battle plans go out the window when the battle begins. Your battle plan was based on the intelligence you had. But once you are engaging in the conflict, the information changes. With it, you must adjust. Sticking to your guns—no pun intended—could actually lose you the battle.

We have seen this time and again with companies failing to act upon new information—sticking to a business model when the market has changed. They lose relevance not because they lost their identity—but because they failed to shift their identity.

There is nothing wrong with being a mission-driven company and celebrating your past. But when a company becomes too concerned with "beating the gospel" of their past, they lose relevance for the present *and* future. Blockbuster, Radio Shack, and Sears are all parables of such failures to shift identity, to change your mind in the face of new information.

As I recuperated and reassessed, some job offers began coming through. One I decided to entertain was MemSQL, which would go through its own identity shift when we changed the name to Sin-gleStore—but more on this later. Fortunately, at this point I had shifted my view of leadership, my view of who I wanted to be.

MemSQL's CEO reached out to me, and I admit I was fascinated with their technology and had some familiarity with their work. A few days later, we met up at the golf club for me to hear more about them.

In many ways, the company checked the boxes I was looking for: As a software database company, they were in the infrastructure space rather than application. Also, he wanted to transition *out* of being CEO, which meant I would not be a Number Two. They were growing but still in their infancy, specifically wanting someone who could help them shape their culture and identity.

It sounded good, and from what I could see, the tech appeared solid. Yet before I was ready to say yes to the opportunity, I needed more information. I had learned my lesson and wanted a full view of who they were, not only what they said about themselves.

So where do you go to gain additional information and insight? The customers.

MemSQL had about sixty customers at the time, and I asked for a list of those I could contact and speak to. In the end, I spoke with twenty-three of them—most of whom are Fortune 500 household names. What would they have to say?

Voice of the Customer

Usually when you reach out to customers for feedback about software, a pattern emerges. Six out of ten will say, "Yes, it's great and works well for us." Two will tell you, "It's epic!" And two more will say, "It's not great, but it works for now."

What amazed me when I met with MemSQL's customers was that I kept hearing the same narrative from all of them:

"We can't do what we do without MemSQL. We've already tried every other database software out there, and it's the best we've seen."

This information, added to what I already knew, made their offer all the more appealing. As I discussed it with friends and colleagues, not everyone was as on board with the idea, though. In fact, in terms of a value proposition, people thought I was crazy to take on the role of CEO at a tenuous start-up.

For instance, MemSQL's financial situation wasn't exactly rosy at the time. While they had some money in the bank, they had only around a six-month runway based on projections of spending and revenue. There were plenty who advised against my taking the position. It felt too risky, especially after what I had just come out of.

I had shared with these individuals the same information I had learned—what the customers said, the financial situation. It was all out on the table. So why did I feel differently than they did when the information was the same?

Context.

My analysis of the information was different than theirs. I agreed it was risky, but at least I knew what the risks were. It's also key to realize that context assigns a different weight to the same information. My friends put more weight on the tenuous financial position of the company. Meanwhile, I put more weight on what MemSQL wanted to accomplish.

In short, I considered how their vision meshed with the concept of real-time analytics. Over and over again, the speed of the software, its accuracy for getting the right information to the right person at the right time, was of greater import to me. The space they were exploring felt well suited to the direction I wanted to take. I could see that such real-time analytics was where the puck was headed.

When you consider world civilizations over the past two millennia, the concept of corporations is still a newer idea, coming about as part of the Industrial Revolution. The rising demand for iron, steel, and oil drove innovation for mechanization, creating efficiencies in production and distribution. The Dale Carnegies and Rockefellers of the era became the first millionaires and had a large influence on the direction of society, especially expectations of the workplace. In time, it became the standard—and then the status quo.

Because of this, some would say the twenty-first century arrived about ten years later than expected with the emergence of smartphones around 2009. Mobile technology forced an identity shift on culture in and out of the workplace, moving us from brick-and-mortar, physical products to a service economy driven through digital spaces.

With this identity shift, there was a corresponding economic shift—from selling goods to selling services. Uber, Apple, Netflix, DoorDash—all are examples of the identity shift.

In a service economy, point-in-time analytics will not suffice. "Just in time" or "delayed" analytics will lead to irrelevancy. If a search result or web page takes longer than three seconds to load, customers move on—probably to your competitor.

The context of business has shifted to one where milliseconds matter. Being in Real Time has severe implications. It gives you a better chance of becoming "future-proof" for the next decade, so long as you continue to innovate.

For instance, if I want to watch a basketball game and also order food, but the food doesn't arrive in time, then the experience I wanted is gone. What are the chances I will order from your restaurant again? Not likely. If this happens enough times, the business cannot survive.

This was the context I saw playing out at MemSQL that ultimately informed my decision in the moment. They were moving customers closer to Real Time with their database analytics. The real-time implications of their software shifted the odds for me.

After all, analysis of information is context itself. The sooner you have context, the sooner you have insight … and the sooner you can make an informed choice.

So I placed my bets on MemSQL and said yes.

New Name, Renewed Purpose

When you make a choice, there are always consequences. The identity shift I chose in becoming CEO of MemSQL wasn't only about the title. Like Steve Rogers, who I was at my core didn't change. But with my identity shift, my responsibilities changed—thus my impact and influence changed.

The main job of the CEO is to be the primary company evangelist. That is, it's your responsibility to give employees a purpose. You can't assume they come in to work with one already. It became very clear to me when joining MemSQL that the company needed more than just a great product. It needed a vision everyone could stand behind, something to differentiate it from the value proposition of the hundreds of other databases available to customers.

For this to happen, you can't just slap nice-sounding words on a page. It has to be a vision the product can fulfill.

Three weeks after joining the company, I gathered the best performers within the company and asked them the same three questions:

"Why do you think certain customers chose MemSQL for their database?"

"Why do you think certain customers chose to leave us for another database?"

"What would you do to put us on a trajectory of growth?"

Their answers to these questions helped me combine Information and Context to then articulate a vision for the company. What became clear was that the database of the future would be one in which customers could transact, analyze, and contextualize data with a response time of milliseconds. These three abilities are exactly what most companies need for AI to work for them.

Once I was clear the product could fulfill this future-proofed vision, I went on a journey to preach the gospel of MemSQL to anyone and everyone—from investors and prospects to my Uber driver. I wanted to get the word out about how we were moving the world closer to Real Time.

Eventually, this prompted an analysis of our company identity. Did the name MemSQL still truly capture who we were? Before I came along, when the company was founded, the focus had been primarily on data storage. The company had still been in its infancy, but just as a baby's personality takes shape as they grow, so the personality of the company had grown. During the pandemic, we realized we needed to rebrand. We needed a refreshed purpose.

Speaking of children, my wife and I love the names we've given to our four children. While we discussed the names together, we had agreed one of us needed the deciding vote each time. Therefore, my wife had the deciding vote for two of our children and I had it for the other two.

I found myself in a similar situation with selecting a new name for the company. Since we had pivoted away from memory-based databases, the name MemSQL was pigeonholing us and not representative of our new vision. We needed a name that would speak to relevancy and recency, as these were our primary value propositions.

The problem was, we had a shoestring budget for rebranding. Saying yes to becoming CEO of MemSQL meant I'd already had to make some very difficult decisions, some of which I'll address in the next chapter, but this included reining in our costs substantially.

We assembled our own branding team to discuss a lot of new names over two months and then eventually narrowed it down to three final contenders. I was given these on a Friday, and the plan was for me to select the final name and announce it on Tuesday.

While thinking the names over, I liked them all, but none of them were making me feel particularly excited. Then, one night as I was brushing my teeth, I had an epiphany. There was a function within our software known as "single store." Essentially, it ensures the data flows from different memory storage destinations to the user based on the recency and relevancy of the data. It was a major differentiator of our software from others because of how it allowed customers to combine transactions and analytics in one platform.

I texted the idea to the company's cofounder. His immediate reaction was to respond, "But that's a feature."

Something I learned from Peter Thiel's book *Zero to One* is that if you're going to succeed, you've got to be right about something that everyone else thinks you're wrong about. Also, you have to be right about it for a *long* time.

So the branding team wasn't very happy with me when I presented my own idea—SingleStore—as the new name instead of any of the suggestions they had labored over. But just like my own children's names, I felt excited about it. In my gut, it felt like the right direction even though the others on the team weren't sure about it. I stuck with my intuition, and to this day, I have no regrets over it.

We couldn't see then how the explosion of generative AI would bode well for our identity shift to SingleStore. It would position us to take advantage of the AI advancements that are now happening in the world. Companies can't truly reap the benefits of AI without real-time analytic databases. It's the single choice a company can make *now* that will have resonance in the future.

Identity Is Action

We often think of identity as a collection of labels we accrue in life—our cultural heritage, religion, political affiliations, and so on. But more than anything else, our identity is rooted in the actions we take.

Consider Steve Rogers again. It's not his appearance or background that makes him Captain America. It's the actions he takes. It's what he fights for that makes him Captain America.

The same is true for all of us. Our identities are made up of memory—the series of Now making up our lives. These are the actions and events we participate in—walking to temple with my grandmother, leaving my PalmPilot in Karen's purse so she would have to connect with me again, spending time with my children on a Saturday morning, swinging a golf club with my father, choosing the name SingleStore even though it was nowhere on the list.

With an identity shift, it is never just a matter of words. It is a matter of action. Seeing the potential of what SingleStore could be, what it could do for the world, is what moved me to join their mission. The potential for making the world more Real Time, more ready for AI, more ready for the future, was irresistible.

> With an identity shift, it is never just a matter of words. It is a matter of action.

This, too, comes back to relevancy. How relevant and how recent the data is empowers a company to be more relevant itself. Speed is of the essence here. It's no longer about the two-second advantage or the two-second disadvantage—we are now looking at the *millisecond* advantage.

For instance, sometimes an investor would come and ask us, "Why does it matter if someone pulls up a report from a database in a couple of seconds rather than milliseconds? Does it truly make that much of a difference?"

We would tell them, "It makes all the difference." Then we would show them that behind every customer interaction, behind every web page refresh, there is a query for data. And since the data is being refreshed often, if you add a couple of seconds to every query in a day, you add on two thousand seconds of wait time for the customer. This is over half an hour of lost time every day.

Add this up every day over the course of weeks and months ... and you begin to see the problem. Lost time. Lost efficiency. Lost resources. Lost customers. Irrelevancy.

Speed is not everything either, though. If you are the fastest on the track but run in the wrong direction, you don't win the race. You become a laughingstock. This is the importance of insight. It allows you to take the right action in the right direction.

Artificial intelligence is the culmination of this journey. The advancements we see through data analysis and creating insight show this to be true. The one who creates insight the fastest wins.

Inaction is not an option. The individuals and companies who take no action will lose their identities, lose their relevance. The ones who *do* take action to become faster—to amplify their intelligence with the tools now available to us—will make the necessary identity shift to survive.

Improvisation

If you challenge conventional wisdom, you will find ways to do things much better than they are currently done.

—MICHAEL LEWIS, QUOTING BILL JAMES, IN
MONEYBALL: THE ART OF WINNING AN UNFAIR GAME

In February of 2020, I had just finished up a meeting and was headed home in an Uber. I felt like I had an ice cube sitting in my chest, and by the time I got home at eight thirty that evening, I felt so sick that I went straight to bed. At two thirty in the morning, I woke up shivering like a leaf, my head burning with a high fever.

I took some Advil but continued to shake uncontrollably. The rest of the night was so horrible, I missed work the next day for the first time in years. I slept in until nine thirty and took my temperature—which was a raging 103 degrees Fahrenheit. As you can imagine, I headed straight to the doctor.

Keep in mind, there had not yet been any reports of COVID-19 reaching the US, so my doctor tested me for the flu. In fact, the thinking at the time was that COVID-19 would be detected by a flu test. Based on this information, he told me, "You don't have COVID, no pneumonia, or flu—just a bad cold."

I continued to feel awful the entire next week, extremely fatigued despite getting extra rest. Since there was no COVID-19 test at the time, I can never be certain I caught the coronavirus, but I'm convinced, based on the experience of others, that this is what happened.

As news reached us about a surge of COVID-19 cases in Korea and East Asia, I returned to work and had to make a decision about our upcoming sales conference. Since there were still no reports of cases in the US, it was decided that we would move forward with holding the conference and adhere to any regulations recommended by health organizations.

The first couple of days of the conference went well, but as reports of COVID-19 in the US escalated, everyone sequestered themselves. By the last day of the kickoff, attendance was anemic at best.

Soon, it was announced that everything but essential services would need to shut down for two weeks to prevent the spread of the illness and overcrowding in hospitals. On Friday, March 13, I got together with a few colleagues to have a steak dinner and enjoy a night out before the quarantine would begin. While I now recognize how foolish this choice was, we made it based on the information and context available at the time. All that was about to change.

The next morning, it looked like a different world when we came down to get into our cars. On the drive home from Half Moon Bay to Los Altos—around a twenty-five-mile drive—we saw only five cars on the road when normally there would have been ten thousand.

The world had been turned upside down. Overnight, everyone had to learn to improvise.

Going against the Stream

A lot has been said about COVID-19 and its impact on the world, especially as it pertains to business. I want to do my best not to retread where others have gone but hopefully present a new perspective. The pandemic created a lot of mess people don't like to talk about—and for good reason. It was a season marked with a lot of loss on multiple fronts.

However, the season of COVID-19 offers some valuable lessons for us in the present if we are courageous enough to look at them. It compelled a lot of improvisation for everyone—from learning how to do school with kids at home to negotiating new distribution channels.

As a rookie CEO at the helm of a fragile tech company, I had no manual for what to do. And the information seemed to change daily. What was supposed to be a two-week quarantine stretched on and on. New regulations came out from the government and from health officials. Meanwhile, companies like ours were having to figure out how to keep working.

Just before the shutdown, one of the moves we had made was to raise the company's debt ceiling to $50 million. We were especially excited about this because it would extend our runway and allow us to shift resources to scaling the company. Almost immediately, the lender reached back out to us and wanted to negotiate the rates due to surplus demand.

The feedback from our investors and partners reflected the conventional wisdom floating around the tech sector—they wanted us to draw down *all* of the $50 million to be a safety net, cut all discretionary spending, and fire 30 percent of the staff.

But the first lesson I learned in the midst of COVID-19 is that you cannot have a herd mentality during a crisis. You should have strong convictions, yes, but held loosely so you can adjust. Because what if everyone is running in the wrong direction? Instead, you need to be your own person. If you need to change direction, you can still improve and adjust. This is much more difficult to do when you're being swept away by the tide.

> You cannot have a herd mentality during a crisis.

We improvised by going in almost the complete opposite direction. While we did cut most of our discretionary spending as advised, we decided against drawing down all of the new debt. Instead, we took only the minimum we needed so we would not be building up an interest problem for ourselves down the road. Even though we had no idea how long the pandemic would go on, we would not make a momentary decision out of fear.

This is what so many companies did wrong in the pandemic. They either froze up with fear and did nothing—or they acted from fear and created worse problems for themselves.

Which leads us to the second lesson I learned from the pandemic: It's okay to swim against the tide. When other companies were experiencing mass layoffs, we signed a pledge to our staff that there would be no layoffs for ninety days. Frankly, we couldn't really afford this kind of pledge, given how we saw our revenue taking a hit. But we decided it was more important to protect the psychological safety of our employees—for them to know they would still have a job for at least three months.

Our hopes were grounded in the sentiment that "this too shall pass." As we all saw during the pandemic, a lot can change in a short time.

A major shift during the pandemic was how data was viewed. Before the pandemic, companies viewed data like the taillights on a car. It was an afterthought. During COVID-19, however, data became the headlights of the car. Companies started to see how valuable data could be to help them see where they needed to go, and none more so than those in the healthcare industry.

As a database company, you would think this would work in our favor. Yet there was one major challenge facing us …

We had not yet fully transitioned to the cloud.

Thriving in the Unknown

Products like Zoom and Microsoft Teams skyrocketed in the early days of the pandemic. After all, with so many people having to work from home, it became a necessity for many businesses.

And while we were nowhere close to a cloud product, many of our customers now found themselves working from home. The beauty of our product was that if a company had a conference room, our solution engineer could go in, set up a computer, and show everyone how to navigate the database to showcase how powerful it was. But if this in-person interaction was taken away—how were we to run our business?

Much has been said about how the pandemic accelerated technology and its use in business. It also exposed where the technological gaps were. For us, it did both of these simultaneously, throwing us into the unknown.

While many kinds of people exist in the world, there are two general categories:

Those who thrive in the known …

… and those who thrive in the unknown.

Start-up life is always a life spent in the unknown the majority of the time. If you can only thrive in the known, then start-up life is not for you.

No matter which category you fall into, the unexpected finds us all. The year 2020 would have been an extremely hard set of circumstances for our family even without COVID-19. My father-in-law had been diagnosed with stage IV cancer in November 2019 and was living with us during his treatment. As you can imagine, the pandemic made hospital visits even more difficult than they already were. Given the precautions, he was often going in for chemotherapy all alone—which caused us immense grief given the little time we had left with him.

Contrast this with my youngest, who was flourishing and full of life at two years old. He wanted nothing more than to go out to the park and play with friends, yet we were telling him we had to stay inside. It felt like we were squashing the spark within him.

For me, it was a reminder of the virtuous cycle of life and its fragility—to see a life blossoming at one end of the house while on the other side, a life was ending.

Tomorrow is not guaranteed for any of us, however. All we have is now. We only have today to take action and change what we can change. Those who say, "We'll do it tomorrow" may never get the chance.

And anyone who did not adapt to digital went away. My colleague's CrossFit gym was a great example of adaptation. They started recording the daily workout and put it up on the app so people could still join from home. They also reduced the price for members, acknowledging the tough times people were experiencing and the loss of the community aspect of CrossFit.

Likewise, restaurants that could not adapt to pickup orders disappeared. The Black Swan event of COVID-19 accelerated years of digital transformation into a matter of months. Those who chose to do nothing and wait for things to get back to "normal" didn't survive.

In short, the pandemic accentuated any weaknesses in a business. This context was made extremely clear when COVID-19 hit. As someone who has thrived when there was a low chance of success, this was a gift to me as a rookie CEO. Extreme adversity builds extreme convictions. It cemented my belief in my own convictions.

For SingleStore, not having a product in the cloud suddenly put us at a disadvantage we were not anticipating. We knew we needed to move to the cloud, but it had been a goal for further down the road. We were focused on viability, but now we had to improvise. It was scary, but in the context of adapting to accommodate a pandemic, it was the only reasonable choice. A database that lacked cloud capabilities was like a restaurant without delivery in the midst of COVID-19—unsustainable.

The Stonecutter

Possibly the greatest lesson we learned through COVID-19 was the value of small, incremental progress. You can't build everything in one day. But you can move one brick and be closer today than you were yesterday. The progress may not always be obvious, but it all adds up in the end.

My favorite analogy for this comes from the late Kobe Bryant, who once said, "When nothing seems to help, I go look at a stonecutter hammering away at his rock perhaps a hundred times without as much as a crack showing in it. Yet at the hundred and first blow it will split in two, and I know it was not that blow that did it, but all that had gone before."[6]

In other words, the rock doesn't break because the 101st blow was so strong—it breaks because of the layers of effort that came before.

---

6   Lee Jenkins, "Lakers Lose Their Rock: Kobe Injury Leaves Massive Void," *Sports Illustrated*, SI.com, April 13, 2013, https://www.si.com/nba/2013/04/13/kobe-bryant-injury-lakers.

In the face of an unexpected crisis that accentuated our software's greatest weakness, we made a choice for incremental progress. Like the hammer on the stone, the change isn't always visible. It doesn't come from one major event that changes everything all at once. Not at all.

Instead, change occurs as a series of small choices, small actions, small debates, energetic conflict, and challenging each other's views to find the best ideas. Each swing of the hammer layers upon the ones that came before until finally the impact is explosive.

COVID-19 taught us that if we kept doing the right actions for a sustained period of time, then goodness would happen.

At the time I'm writing this book, we have grown from sixty customers to around three hundred. While I believe this is because our product is the best on the market, this is not the only reason for our success. It's the choice to keep hammering away, to layer progress incrementally until the rock breaks.

There have been times when I've been asked by an interviewer, "What is the one thing you did to get here?" But the truth is, there is no "one thing." There is no single hire, no customer win, no product launch that made success on its own. Life is often two steps forward, one step back. What adds up to success is the choice to put two steps forward after the step back. This is what sets apart the successful start-ups.

There is no silver bullet to success. It's a series of Now. A series of choosing to improvise when necessary, to swing the hammer even when it seems that nothing is happening.

Improvising the Experience

There is always a risk in improvisation. Yet it is often the secret ingredient in what differentiates you from the rest of the crowd. It is what creates an experience people will cling to. But is there a metric to use to know if you're improvising the right way?

I believe there is.

At home in California, I never take a taxi. If I'm not driving myself, I'm taking an Uber. The same is true when I visit New York. I probably haven't used a taxi there in five years, because the experience is dreadful. I could say the same for Paris or any other city you could name.

Save one: London.

When I visit London, I never use Uber. I always use a London taxi. What makes the difference?

As Uber swept the world a few years ago, taxi companies were the hardest hit. Uber had changed customer expectations. While many taxi companies tried to fight back through having Uber banned or making it difficult to become an Uber driver, the London cab drivers took a different approach. They improvised.

They realized a fundamental business truth: "We have to become a better product than Uber."

It may sound like an exaggeration, but it may be more difficult to become a London taxi driver than becoming a CEO. They have made the process exhaustive on purpose because they wanted the London cab experience to be better than Uber in every respect.

People who want to be a taxi driver in London have to walk the entire city. In fact, the training they must complete is referred to as "The Knowledge." They must know every nook and cranny of the city—and as a result, today's London taxicab driver is more courteous and educated than they were ten years ago.

If I get into an Uber in London and ask the driver about a building, ten to one they can tell me. Actually, those odds are generous in my experience. In the off times I've given Uber a chance in London, the drivers either knew too little English to answer or shrugged and said, "I don't know."

Meanwhile, if I ask a London taxi driver about a certain building, they will know its name and its history. They are incredibly knowledgeable about their city, making the experience far superior. With this approach, they have managed to win against Uber—not by putting Uber down as other cities tried but by offering a superior product.

To know whether you are improvising the right way or not, the secret is this: you must consider the user experience.

Ultimately, the key to creating a superior product is the user experience. Consider Sony's Betamax player from the 1980s. It was arguably the better-designed product from a technological view. But VHS was the more user-friendly product and won the market. History is filled with great products left behind, leapfrogged by a "lesser" product. The user experience always casts the deciding vote, and is always about the latest context. That is, are you meeting the user's expectations *today?* This is also the power of Now.

As a digital company, Uber could shift the London experience if they wanted to. They could put historical data in the app so their drivers could have knowledge similar to the taxi drivers. But to this day, they have not yet done so.

Likewise, when evolving your product or service, it's not about how many bells and whistles you can add. It's about the experience the customer has. You may recall that this was the deciding factor for me to become CEO of SingleStore—the reported customer experience.

This was the final lesson learned from the pandemic. Put people first—your team and your customers. I believe our success today was because when we were forced to improvise, we chose to put people first. Your ability to pivot, to create an excellent experience, to improve each day—these are what will future-proof you.

It will be the same with generative AI. It's an iterative process, a continuous swinging of the hammer. The companies who can implement AI to create a better experience, to help them improvise with more insight, will be the ones who thrive. To get there, they will have to leverage the power of Now—wielding the right Information in the right Context for the right Choice.

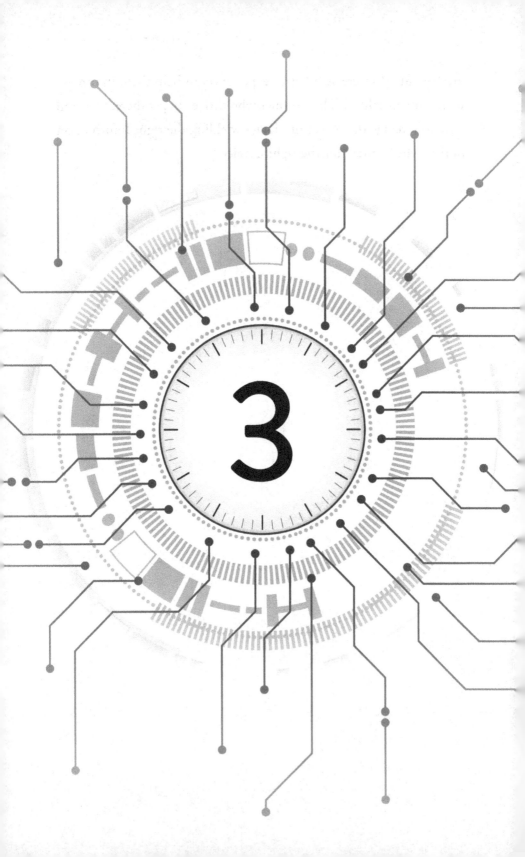

WHERE
WE
ARE
GOING

A Great Escape

Man is nothing else but what he purposes, he exists only in so far as he realizes himself, he is therefore nothing else but the sum of his actions, nothing else but what his life is.

—JEAN-PAUL SARTRE, FRENCH PHILOSOPHER

At long last, we've arrived here—the future. If there is any one lesson I've learned from my past, it's that the future is always a bit foggy. It encapsulates the unknown. As such, the future can cause feelings of fear or thrill—like a roller coaster. Sometimes it is difficult to untangle the two.

But the choices you make today—in the Now—can provide great clarity to what the future holds. Though the decisions we made at SingleStore during COVID-19 were counterintuitive, they did much to clarify the company's future. We built on our base and extended the runway.

The name change from MemSQL to SingleStore also further clarified what we wanted our future to look like, how it needed to differentiate from our past. As I mentioned in the last chapter, I had no idea this name change would bode well for our future. With generative AI exploding into the mainstream ethos, the value of having fast and accurate data has become more apparent than ever. The idea of having a single database to not only store data but illuminate through the power of context holds great ramifications for how a business makes decisions.

Which is why we must now dive deeper into the role of Context within Now—and specifically, how it shapes the future. As Khalil Gibran wrote in his poem "On Time," "Yesterday is but today's memory, and tomorrow is today's dream."

While we can certainly learn from the past, we should be wary of overindexing on its importance to making decisions about the future. Jeff Bezos once expressed this sentiment by observing, "The death knell for any enterprise is to glorify the past—no matter how good it was."

Why? Because there is no homeostasis in Now. It is always on the move. Today is a much better predictor of the future than yesterday. But literally everything can change in an *instant*.

One of the days now permanently etched in my brain is March 9, 2023. I had an 8:00 a.m. tee time and was hosting a customer for a round at my golf club. During breakfast, I briefly read a headline about a misstep made by Silicon Valley Bank, but it didn't seem like that big a news story at the time. I assumed its stock would get hammered for a bit and then it would eventually bounce back.

The round started off a bit rainy, but the day grew lovely as we went on. I'd left my phone stowed in the locker room so I could be fully invested in the present moment with our customer, enjoying the natural energy of the course and our conversation.

Afterward, I stepped off the golf course, shaking off the competitive energy and enjoying the cool breeze of the afternoon. My phone buzzed back to life in the locker room where I had left it a few hours before, and the first message to catch my eye was from Brad Kinnish, our CFO. It read, "We will make payroll."

On its own, the statement was innocuous. *We always make payroll*, I thought as I put my shoes back on. With over $200 million in the bank at the time, payroll had not been close to the top of my concerns, so why was Brad texting me this news?

Then my ears caught a stray comment by a fellow golfer from across the locker room. "Did you hear about the run on Silicon Valley Bank (SVB)?"

In a split second, I now had the *context* of Brad's payroll message, and a chill went down my spine. What had happened?

As I got on the phone with Brad, I learned the full story of what had transpired. Apparently, SVB had invested in ten-year mortgages, but when the housing market rates went up, this resulted in a staggering $1.8 billion loss on its bond portfolio. To make up the deficit, it announced a plan to sell stock to raise $2.25 billion. This news led to a downgrade of SVB's long-term local currency bank deposit and issuer ratings by Moody's.

This was the financial equivalent of a deadly, raging wildfire. The bank was home to more than twenty-five hundred venture capital firms, and the news spread like embers on a gusty day. The fear was palpable. VCs had begun pulling their funds late on Wednesday, and now start-ups were following suit, withdrawing their funds as soon as the news broke.

In the span of four to six hours, SVB saw $42 billion withdrawn. I don't care who you are—no bank can survive this kind of run. And it truly was a "run" on the bank, as its website went down in the process and CFOs were literally jumping into cars and driving to the physical bank to withdraw money in person—a nearly unthinkable scenario in the present age of almost immediate digital transactions.

SVB, the sixteenth-largest bank in the US, was on the brink of collapse. The implications were devastating. Start-ups with their entire funds in SVB faced an existential crisis. Without access to their accounts, they couldn't pay their employees or their bills. They were staring at the possibility of going out of business overnight—and by no fault of their own.

By the next morning, it was announced the bank was in receivership. It was unthinkable that a financial institution that had been at the heart of Silicon Valley, a bastion of innovation for forty years, would crash within the course of a single day like a modern Greek tragedy.

The information in the headlines had created a new financial context within milliseconds. The ensuing choices by VCs and start-ups to withdraw their funds added gasoline to the fire. And SVB was left in ashes.

Context Is King

In the grand tapestry of life, from the moment we draw our first breath, we begin to amass an astronomical collection of data points. Trillions of transactional data points between our neurons, if you will. Yet this staggering sum of information stands idle, a dormant titan, unless bestowed with the gift of context.

The importance of context in decision-making cannot be understated. When you compare the collapse of SVB to the global financial crisis (GFC) of 2008, a clear story emerges—the speed of information has changed the current business context we find ourselves in. In a matter of hours, your legacy can be wiped from the face of the earth because of a single misstep.

In the pre-Twitter world, it's doubtful this would have happened with the same rapidity. With the GFC, the devastation was like a staggered domino effect. There were even bankers who saw it coming, but because of how the system was structured, they had no power to stop it once the first dominoes toppled. While it was still devastating, its effects were felt over a period of time, spread out. Some businesses were better able to mitigate the impact than others.

With SVB, the real-time impact of nearly instantaneous information could be seen in full force. And, of course, this impacted not only SVB but all the Silicon Valley businesses with accounts in the bank. Some businesses that had most of their holdings in SVB suddenly found themselves in a position in which they could not access their funds—they *wouldn't* make payroll. This fact provided me with the context I needed for Brad's text message.

In fact, let's return to that pivotal moment when my brain was flooded with this profound context. Moments later, I was ensnared in conversation with Brad, my ears ringing with the unfolding saga of SVB's downfall. As he spoke, my heart pounded with raw, unfiltered horror.

As Brad spoke, it became clear to me that we had managed to remain unscathed while being in the thick of this catastrophe. We had dodged a potentially fatal bullet.

So how did SingleStore, which had about $200 million in cash, not get affected by the SVB collapse? Why were we able to make payroll while thousands of people were at risk of losing their livelihoods in a few hours?

It all comes down to how Information with Context helps each one of us make Choices.

The Sum of Our Actions

At the time of their collapse, SingleStore had only $1.2 million in Silicon Valley Bank, which we effectively treated as our checking account for daily expenses. The rest of our money was safe in a money market account (MMA) backed by US government securities.

The previous November, SVB had approached us about the idea of moving all of our money over to them. The incentive was that they would offer us a higher interest rate, which would conceivably net an additional $1 million a year for us. It was certainly worth considering, as we were actively looking for ways to make our money work harder for us.

Our ultimate decision came down to Brad's judgment as CFO. While it was an attractive offer, he felt that keeping our money in the federally backed MMA was a less risky choice—even though we would net less from the interest rate. In this decision, Brad exemplified the sort of risk-mitigation mindset that sets apart great leaders. For him, it was about the context of where the money was. Simply put, Brad preferred the credit risk of the US government over SVB.

When we declined SVB's offer, they took it well, but they also couldn't believe we would turn down the higher rate they were offering. They felt we were being a little overparanoid by keeping our money divided, especially given their solid reputation in the Silicon Valley community.

In hindsight, Brad's decision was partly informed by a piece of timeless wisdom: "Don't put all your eggs in one basket." Yet the moment of choice was more than this. It was his strong sense of fiduciary duty and desire to de-risk our money. His decision was reinforced by the learnings from the GFC that no institution is too big to fail. In fact, if you want to look at it in terms of a database, you could see this contextualization of the past as transactional information stored in his brain, aiding him in making an informed choice.

After all, we were certainly not the only start-up being offered the same deal. And I have no doubt many others jumped at the opportunity to move their money over and earn the higher interest rate. We had the same information available to us as any other Silicon Valley entity, yet we applied a different context in choosing how we wanted to steward our funds.

While our memory makes up our identity, our choices determine who we *will* be. As Sartre said when referring to the human condition, we are the sum of our actions—or choices, if you will. Our decisions now are an act of choosing our own future. Context changes *everything*.

The Building Blocks of Intelligence

A surprising savior emerged in the aftermath of SVB's collapse. In an unanticipated move, the federal government declared it would shield all corporate funds held with the fallen institution. This intervention, while not obligatory, may have single-handedly averted a catastrophic ripple effect through the technology industry—and the wider economy.

Essentially, this means that even if we had kept all our money in SVB, by the following Tuesday, we would have been in the clear. But I slept better that weekend knowing we would lose only $1.2 million at worst. Our people would still be able to show up to work and put food on their tables.

This act of salvation became a topic of discussion between Madhukar Kumar, our chief marketing officer, and me during our annual sales meeting in San Diego. As immigrants who had found success in the cutthroat world of Silicon Valley, we reflected on the role of choices in our journey. We marveled at how decisions made by others had shaped the landscape for countless entrepreneurs and engineers who came after them.

Over dinner, I turned to Madhukar and proposed an idea: "If we can encapsulate our thoughts and feelings about this in words, we should take out a full-page ad in the *Wall Street Journal*." The caveat was that it had to genuinely represent our collective sentiment as a company.

We continued our conversation on the walk back from dinner, with the idea still percolating in my mind. By the time I woke up the next morning, the script for the ad was waiting for me. A few tweaks later, it was ready. We decided to take the leap and place the ad, even going so far as to leave a copy of the newspaper on every seat at the sales kickoff meeting the following morning.

This sequence of events was a symphony of Information, Context, and Choice, resonating not just within our company but throughout the interconnected web of the tech industry.

Choices, I realized, are not solitary phenomena. They ripple outward, influencing not just our own reality but the realities of others. The adoption of an abandoned child, the acceptance of my grand-mother into my family—these choices made decades ago continue to shape the lives of my daughters today, granting them opportunities they might not otherwise have had.

Choices are not made in a vacuum. They are the product of Information and Context, the raw materials from which we construct our identities.

The more I pondered this idea, the more it struck me how, in many ways, companies mirror the complexity of individuals. They are conglomerates of people, each with their own Information, Context, and Choice. This trifecta is what differentiates one company from another, even when they operate in the same market with similar products and services.

In essence, Information, Context, and Choice are not only the pillars that make up Now—they are also the building blocks of *intelligence*. When we apply this thinking to both human intelligence and artificial intelligence, we can begin the process of demystifying how we can create insight, how we shape our identities through our choices, and how we build the future we want.

Silicon Valley is not a location. It is an idea.

It is a melting pot where everyone speaks the same language — the language of innovation.

Silicon Valley is an actualization of dreams. And a conviction of notions.

It is an emotion that starts with a "what if" and ends with a change.

It is a tapestry of tenacity and a fusion of sweat, tears, laughter, and ringing the bell.

Silicon Valley is sometimes a graveyard of ideas yet a fertile ground that blooms a thousand creations.

It is a valley of the boom. And sometimes a trough of the bust.

Silicon Valley is not a bank.

It is an institution. A tradition of invention. A collective where strangers bank on each others' ideas.

To this idea, to this melting pot, to this emotion that is Silicon Valley, we say — Dream on!

May the best ideas thrive and give birth to a thousand more.

Silicon Valley is a place we are proud to call home .

www.singlestore.com

Demystifying AI

A year spent in artificial intelligence
is enough to make one believe in God.

—ALAN PERLIS, COMPUTER SCIENTIST AND
FIRST RECIPIENT OF THE TURING AWARD

We find ourselves in a fast-moving, fast-changing world where every week brings a new announcement about tech, new noise around AI, or a new company or product being launched into the world. With each passing Now, the landscape is being augmented, and it's easy to get lost. With AI, we've seen a sensory overload that has caused individuals and organizations alike to jump to various conclusions.

The conversation around AI has become like the old analogy of three blind men touching different parts of an elephant. No one has the full picture. Unfortunately, all too often half knowledge is worse than no knowledge.

If we keep a foggy, narrow lens through which the view of AI is not well informed or well rounded, we will lose our way in the landscape.

Therefore, I want to spend the majority of this chapter demystifying artificial intelligence. With AI, we must take a high-level view, because you have to rise above the noise if you want to see the horizon.

Also, it should be noted that the view I present here is my view and the SingleStore view of AI. While I shall attempt to paint an unbiased view of the AI landscape, obviously I have a biased context for why we feel the database solutions we've built are well suited to what the future holds.

After all, if you want to take advantage of the AI advancements happening in the world, you need a robust database to do so. Having a database that can handle the storage, access, and contextualization of data is of great consequence here. It is the one single action you can take now that resonates into the future. It allows you to defog the future and to gain the two-*millisecond* advantage. Without it, you cannot create insight—you cannot shift your identity to adapt to changes. Without it, you cannot make the most informed choice possible.

To make AI meaningful, you have to look beyond the technology itself and consider the *impact*. The technology is no more than the packaging; therefore, it's not enough to look at it as another tool for efficiency or automation. We have to look at the opportunity for artificial intelligence to *amplify* intelligence.

Breaking Down AI

Stack Overflow has long been the proverbial "watering hole" for developers—a thriving hub where engineers could share their coding conundrums and collectively troubleshoot. It's a place where the community's collective wisdom is greater than the sum of its parts, where questions can be tagged as duplicates or solutions proposed. Over the years, this site has become a treasure trove of transactional data—a living, breathing testament to the evolution of coding practices, platforms, and tools.

And then, in the blink of an eye, the landscape changed. With the advent of ChatGPT in late 2022, the once-bustling Stack Overflow saw a precipitous drop in traffic. At the time of writing, it was decreasing by an alarming 6 percent per month.

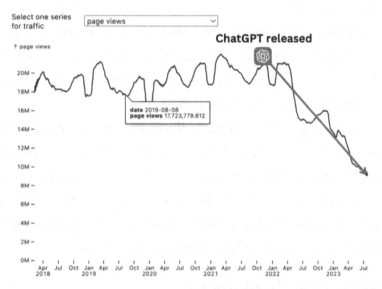

In hindsight, it's easy to rationalize this shift. Developers now had a new tool in their arsenal that allowed them to troubleshoot and code *simultaneously*. With GitHub Copilot and ChatGPT, the need to open a new browser window and navigate to Stack Overflow was eliminated.[7]

7   Des Darilek, "Insights into Stack Overflow Traffic," LinkedIn, accessed August 18, 2023, https://www.linkedin.com/posts/tom-alder_the-irony-is-crushing-stack-overflows-activity-7099208596369903616-EQH6/?utm_source=share&utm_medium=member_desktop.

But here's where the story takes an interesting turn. Chat GPT-4, the brainchild of OpenAI, had been trained on publicly available data up until September 2021. This data, allegedly, included the same billions of transactions that Stack Overflow had been diligently collecting and analyzing.

Then why did the same data in the hands of OpenAI lead to such a seismic shift in the coding landscape? What did OpenAI do differently with the same information that Stack Overflow had been sitting on for years?

And this is where our investigation begins about how to define and demystify AI.

It begins with Context, as introduced in the last chapter. Context is an alchemist, transforming this raw, unprocessed data into a powerful tool for decision-making. Some might even argue that context is the linchpin, the very essence of everything.

This principle holds true not only for we humans but also for the realm of software and large language models (LLMs). This is where OpenAI can put millions of code error stack into the context of what a developer is trying to do and help solve an issue or create new code in a few seconds. Stack Overflow had the data, but it was OpenAI that took the data and added context to create action.

Information Is Identity

When we contemplate AI, we are truly contemplating ourselves. The essence of our quest for artificial intelligence is a mirror in many ways. It reflects back our own cognitive processes, our own intelligence. It's not a simple reflection, though—it's a complex, multidimensional one, revealing not just how we think but how we remember.

Our lives, from the moment we open our eyes in the morning to the moment we close them at night, are a symphony of memory storage and recall. These memories, so deeply woven into the fabric of our identities, often operate on a subconscious level. This is the realm of muscle memory, where actions become automatic, requiring no conscious thought.

For instance, consider the ease with which you tie your shoes while conversing with a family member. There's no need to question who this person is or what the strange objects on your feet are. Action and thought become woven together seamlessly in the moment.

Yet for those who have had to watch Alzheimer's disease slowly erase the memories of their loved ones, the importance of memory becomes painfully clear. Until such a devastating loss, it's easy to take it for granted. Our memory, it seems, *is* our identity.

To define AI, we need to first recognize that data and memory play a key role in how we currently define human intelligence. Only then can we go down the hypothetical path of recreating intelligence through a machine.

At its core, memory is a ceaseless stream of data points. Every moment of our lives, we gather information, store it in the seemingly bottomless storage of our brains, and then access the information in milliseconds as needed.

Side note: at SingleStore, we offer a feature called "bottomless storage" for our customers … but I digress.

So at what point does information become knowledge?

Much like the human brain's synapses and neurons, the data we collect is connected to each other. When our brains discover a pattern in this data and how it is connected, the raw data elevates to knowledge. The more experiences and learnings we have, the more "knowledgeable" we become.

However, just like a large library of books, the sheer collection of data points doesn't make us intelligent. We also have "weights" associated with the connections of the data points to help us know how they relate to one another—in other words, the importance of knowing that a history lesson we learned in school is connected to a movie we are watching in real time. We need another component that can add a layer of meaning to all our collected Information.

The data points that we incessantly and perpetually collect vary from moment to moment. Our memory could be about the awe-inspiring sight of a sunset, the tension of a difficult conversation, or the soaring sense of camaraderie felt while sharing a beer with a colleague. Before these experiences are filed away in the recesses of our minds, though, we add in the additional layer with these data points.

We add *Context*.

Enter Context

With Context, our brain attaches emotions, thoughts, and lessons together. We are also selective in what we choose to remember. For example, you might not recall what you wore two days ago, but perhaps you can describe in vivid detail the outfit you wore the day you met your significant other or best friend. The context colors and shapes the memory—it triages what is vital from what is forgettable.

In turn, our memories then shape our reality. Our reality is experienced through our memories—bits and bytes of transactional data *with* context. It's a ceaseless cycle, a perpetual dance of existence.

We effectively live in an incessant cycle of Now. What makes us different from each other, even if we live through the same experience, is the context of every single piece of data we process. The last piece of the puzzle that brings Information and Context into action is *Choice*.

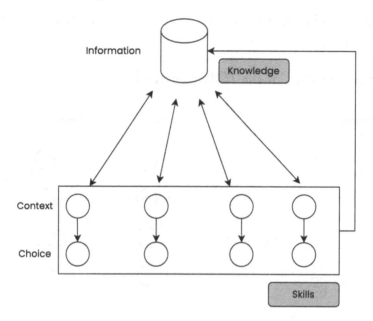

Choice Is Action

When Information and Context come together, we can make Choices that align with actions. Repeated action leads to the building of skills, which is often referred to as muscle memory.

For example, using my memory or information I have stored about a basketball game, I can notice a pattern of outcomes, which informs my actions. It is what allows me to develop the muscle memory to dribble the basketball instead of kicking it like a soccer ball.

A good outcome helps us store that information with context so there is more incentive in repeating those actions based on patterns. Over time, the repeated actions become our skills.

It's not so different with AI—repetition of an action makes it more intelligent with each iteration, forming a type of "digital muscle memory." With additional information and context, prediction improves, insight is created, and choices themselves become more intelligent.

It is this combination of Information, Context, and Choice that forms the building blocks of a framework we call the Trinity of Intelligence (TOI).

The Three Pillars of the TOI Framework

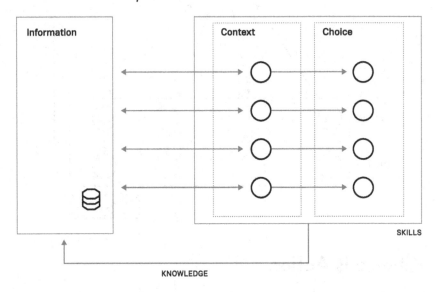

The Trinity of Intelligence Framework to Demystify AI

To illustrate this framework's potential, let's consider a fictional multinational corporation—Acme Bank. At the Information stage, the bank's platform processes copious amounts of financial, operational, and customer data—identifying subtle correlations and nascent trends. Next, as the bank grapples with the nuances of globalization, the platform's Context layer tailors insights to regional markets' unique preferences and regulatory environments.

Ultimately, the final touchstone of Choice emerges as Acme Bank leverages the AI-powered recommendations, including automating logistics, elucidating marketing endeavors, and enhancing its financial outlook. All three pillars—Information, Context, and Choice—play integral roles in the bank's transformative journey, underscoring the TOI framework's relevance in guiding businesses through the AI landscape.

In embracing the foundational pillars of Information, Context, and Choice, the TOI framework delineates a multidimensional path for translating AI potential into tangible outcomes. Seizing the opportunities lying at the intersection of these pillars, organizations can unravel the mysterious tapestry of artificial intelligence and devise strategies that harmonize technology and human intelligence.

The framework illuminates the pathway toward intelligent, context-aware decision-making. As it does, it foreshadows the evolution of businesses into resilient, adaptive, and competitive entities wielding AI as both compass *and* catalyst.

Now, let's look at a large language model (LLM), one of the building blocks of AI. Typically, an LLM is a binary file that has stored data points (parameters) and connects the similar data points with weights to signify the importance of the connections between each point. For example, the words *boy, prince,* and *king* may be connected more closely to each other than to the words *girl, princess,* and *queen* In other words, it has context to apply to the information.

When asked to answer a question about the data points an LLM has been trained on, it works to answer the query by *predicting* the next word. It does so by mimicking the patterns that already exist in the data connections. The larger the number of parameters, the more "knowledgeable" the LLM is considered.

This is the reason we have model names with parameters—for example, Llama2 7B, 13B, or 70B parameters. When the model parameters are extremely large, the prediction of the next word and the word after becomes sentences that are not just *syntactically* true but also *semantically* correct. Sometimes, however, when the words are predicted and connected together, the response may not be true, yet it matches the pattern of existing data the model has been trained on. When this happens, it's called "hallucination."

When the same action happens on a different set of data—for instance, a photo or illustration or even audio and video—the generation of new data becomes the seed of creativity that has taken the world by storm since OpenAI's release of its LLM ChatGPT.

As humans, we have been trying to build machine learning (ML) models like this for a very long time. As part of the process, we pick a dataset, let the model learn the patterns (training), give it a new dataset to make predictions (inference), and then evaluate the results.

However, OpenAI made a key addition to this process that took the world by surprise in the results they started seeing after adding billions of parameters for training. That addition is called reinforcement learning with human feedback (RLHF). When the ChatGPT model was being tested, its results were refined by humans to tell the LLM what was a good response and which ones were bad. This process is now called *alignment*, and much has been written about it recently.

The use of RLHF and the process of alignment was the major breakthrough that brought OpenAI and LLMs to the forefront with ChatGPT.

By predicting the next data point (words, sentences, audio, video, etc.), LLMs have now developed a few key skills that can be applied to a wide range of use cases. These skills include generation, summarization, translation, and analysis.

Generation is essentially the completion of words and practically any information based on the data it has been trained on. This means we can use LLMs for generating content, articles, images, sound, videos, and—very importantly—code. With code generation, we can now use LLMs to build applications to assist human developers.

Summarization can be used for taking a large amount of data and then condensing it to a few data points without losing any meaning of the entire data.

Translation, on the other hand, can be used to translate words from one language to another—or translating words into images or videos or vice versa. One example of this is that of DALL-E, which is capable of translating text prompts into images.

When it comes to analysis, we can use LLMs to analyze patterns in data that would otherwise be missed. Instead of using LLMs like a simple knowledge database—such as an encyclopedia—we can also use it for *reasoning*. For example, our fictional Acme Bank could input a bunch of text and numbers into an LLM and ask it to do a sentiment analysis or find insights into customer behaviors. From this analysis, the bank can then determine modifications to its banking app or develop new products and services. We ourselves found this application quite useful. In fact, you are welcome to check out a demo we created of LLM analysis with the OpenAI plug-in for SingleStore.

In many ways, an LLM is a personification of the TOI framework. The transactional data points (parameters) are collected over a period of time, connected with weights to embed patterns (training) and context to make these models knowledgeable. Finally, by getting reinforcements from humans via RLHF, it develops skills to execute actions, such as predicting the next data point.

However, there is one missing piece we need to consider when it comes to using LLMs within enterprises. The models have no knowledge about the exabytes of data within companies, so how do we provide them the right context at the right time to help them make the right predictions (choices)?

What follows below uses the TOI framework to build a blueprint for building enterprise-grade LLM solutions.

Building on the TOI framework, our team has developed a blueprint architecture for enterprise AI that you can freely use to make your own choices. In short, it's a blueprint for companies to understand and master AI through data. You can delve deeper into this topic and download the blueprint from timeisnow.ai.

Amplifying Intelligence

Throughout this book, we have returned consistently to the concept of the three pillars of Now—Information (memory), Context (analysis), and Choice (decision). Like individuals, organizations also have brains for storing their collective knowledge. If we think of artificial intelligence as being like a brain, it becomes easier to understand.

The brain has three key layers that are always interacting with one another to drive our decision-making processes. Likewise, AI can be understood through these three layers:

- Layer 1: Interfaces—receptors and effectors
- Layer 2: Prefrontal cortex—models and tools
- Layer 3: Memory and context—analysis of transactional data

Exactly how the brain works remains one of the great mysteries of life. It's also a little bit of a mystery how exactly AI works. Yet by taking a closer look at each of these layers, we can not only demystify AI but demystify how we as humans make decisions.

Layer 1: Interfaces

The first layer is made up of interfaces—that is, the receptors and effectors. Think of these as the nerve receptors that are taking in all the information from throughout the body—especially the input of our five senses. These interfaces directly interact with the outside world, taking in a constant stream of data occurring in real time.

The AI equivalent for this is the interface used by the human to provide the system with the information it needs to work. Examples would be conversational UIs (user interfaces) such as a chatbot used on a website or app for a customer service issue. Voice assistants like Alexa or Siri also fit in here. It's a piece of technology that is designed for human interaction.

Within tech, these interfaces help us understand the work without having to understand everything happening within the tech. You don't need to see a website's algorithm to search for a product. The interface brings you only what is most relevant so you can take action.

Not all information an interface interacts with will prove useful, which is why it does not drive action on its own. For instance, you do not act on every ad that pops up online because not all of them are relevant to you. You have other layers of your brain that help you decide whether to take action. The interface's job is to gather input and receive feedback.

Likewise, companies have a layer of interfaces to interact with their stakeholders, whether they are customers, employees, or investors. In the wake of the pandemic, as the view of data has shifted from being the taillights to the headlights, companies are wrestling with how to collect new data. Understanding this first layer is key to ensuring you collect the right data to drive decision-making.

What interfaces do you have in place now? Which ones do you need to ensure you are taking in the right information? Technology can amplify human capabilities here.

For instance, the sense of touch is a human interface. I can check the temperature of the meat I'm cooking with my finger, but I could get burned. Better that I use a meat thermometer, which will not only keep me safe but give me a far more accurate reading of the temperature than my finger alone can do. This allows me to make a better choice on how long to keep cooking.

It's no different with creating insight through your interfaces. Whether you utilize conversational UI chatbots, browser plug-ins for data collection, widgets, or audio/video interfaces, the purpose of these tools is to interact in real time with the real world to gather input and also respond in multiple formats.

The information collected here does not meet a dead end. It must have a channel from which decisions can be made. This leads us to the next layer—the prefrontal cortex.

Layer 2: Prefrontal Cortex

In the human brain, the prefrontal cortex is responsible for regulating our thoughts, actions, and even our emotions by applying intelligence. In other words, it's what keeps us from acting only upon instinct. When you pull back your hand from a hot surface, it's instinctual. Your body acts without the input of the prefrontal cortex. It's the same with breathing or any number of biological functions that keep us alive.

But when you sit down at a restaurant and you're handed a menu, your prefrontal cortex is activated to make decisions based on the input coming from the two other layers of your brain. It says, "My receptors are telling me I'm not very hungry at the moment. However, my memory is telling me the portions here are smaller and that the wait time is a bit longer since everything is made fresh." These pieces of information will help inform your choice when the server returns.

In addition, context is also weighing in. Context may tell you, "Since I'm eating with a romantic partner and not a business client, I should get additional input on what they like or if they have any allergies."

With this flow of information from Layer 1 and Layer 3, the prefrontal cortex is able to make a more informed decision on what you should order. As such, it can handle massive amounts of data with intersecting layers of meaning and context.

Within the scope of AI, this "prefrontal cortex" is composed of the models and tools performing the work. While decision-making looks different with artificial intelligence than the human kind, it's still making choices based on the parameters of the model or tool. Without these, it would be incapable of giving any kind of meaningful results.

For instance, if you were to prompt ChatGPT for a short blog about how a combustion engine works and it sent back a recipe for carrot cake, you would likely be disappointed. Unless, of course, you love carrot cake and can make use of the recipe later.

The LLMOps occurring within ChatGPT are performing the work of the prefrontal cortex. They are using the information from the interface, combined with the memory and context, to decide which information to give you. When the model works correctly, it sends back the relevant information through the interface so you can make use of it.

You then have the opportunity through the interface to refine what it sent. You might prompt it, "Can you now give me a couple of paragraphs about the difference between gas combustion engines and diesel combustion engines?"

No matter how robust this layer of the AI is, however, it can do nothing without the two layers around it. If there is no interface to give it input, it has no reason to make a decision. If it has no memory or context to draw from, its decisions will be either too narrow or too confusing to be useful.

Companies also have a prefrontal cortex to drive their decision-making. They have processes, regulations, organizational structures, standards, and best practices—all of these are models and tools that help an organization make choices. The corporate brain, like the human brain and artificial intelligence, is only as good as its input. When a company relies only on memory and has no interface, it will lose relevance. When it only has interface and no context or memory, then it will chase every trend and be relevant for no one.

The prefrontal cortex's greatest strength is its ability to process all the information coming in and out of it from the other two layers. So it is with AI, which is where we must then turn our attention to the third layer.

Layer 3: Memory and Context

As discussed before, our memory makes up our identity. When we interact with the world, our brains store the memories generated from our experiences. But if you erase the memory of a person—if they experience amnesia or dementia—it erases their very identity and sense of who they are.

Few of us can perfectly recite the exact dates of key historical events, yet we dedicate extra memory to the birth dates of our loved ones. It appears I've passed on my exceptional memory to two of my four children. My youngest, who is six years old at the time of this writing, is a walking sports database. You can ask him about a myriad of teams in various sports, and he can rattle off their full roster. It's uncanny.

Imagine for a moment the feeling you have when you see a familiar face but you struggle to recall the correct name. You might grit your teeth, begin to sweat, and hope they either go speak with someone else or that you luck out and overhear their name. Why? Because the embarrassment of not remembering their name can quickly cause damage to your credibility.

On the flip side, imagine the impact of the moment you're able to recall not only the person's name but also other details to ask, "How is your oldest doing in volleyball? Is your spouse still enjoying their new job?" They feel cared for and seen, and it builds your credibility with them.

It's no different with companies. The faster you can pull up data with relevancy and recency, the better for AI. The core of AI is data. The tool itself is irrelevant without it. The longer it takes AI to get the relevant data, the further away you move from Real Time. This is where milliseconds matter and why at SingleStore we have had a laser focus on ensuring that our database gets the right information to the right person at the right time. Because if you can do this, you can solve any problem in the world.

For companies, every customer interaction, transaction, sales report, vision meeting, and mission statement represents the bits and bytes of data forming your corporate identity. Erase it, and all you have left is corporate amnesia—a name detached from identity. In the midst of writing this book, Twitter became X, and Overstock. com bought the brand identity of Bed Bath & Beyond. It will be interesting to see how these identity shifts play out.

New memories are made in part through the first layer—the interfaces. Relying on historical data alone will also lead to irrelevancy. Imagine if Google Maps only used data from when it was first launched in 2005. No one would use it. Or if they did, they would end up lost.

In the technological sphere, this is why a database is so essential. It makes up the memory of an organization, which makes up its identity. If the information is not stored and accessible, then it bears no weight toward the identity of the company.

Not only that—a smart database does more than simply serve as storage. Like human memory, it knows which data points to discard, which to emphasize, and how to filter the information through context.

For example, if I ask a customer database to pull up customers with the first name "John" without context, it will just give me an alphabetized list of Johns. This might take hours for you to go through.

With context applied, an intelligent database has the intuition to know not to bring me every John in its system but just the most relevant ones for me. It promotes the most recent exchanges to the top of the search results. It might recognize that I've interacted with only two Johns in the past week and therefore predict I am trying to reach one of those two. This increases your efficiency to make a decision and take action.

Ultimately the goal is to be intelligent at all three levels of the brain. But if you have to pick one where you have the greatest level of control—it's here. The intelligence of the database amplifies the intelligence occurring in the AI model, which in turn amplifies the intelligence of the feedback sent back through the interface.

The Human Element

At SingleStore, this third layer is not only the work I lead as CEO of SingleStore—it's the foundation for *everyone's* work moving forward. It is here in the database where Information, Context, and Choice all meet. It is the dividing line between relevance and irrelevance. It empowers the Now.

How you respond to a situation is not so different from how an LLM works. It's based on your own experiences—your personal database. As people, we are largely determined by our responses to impetus. If you were brought up in a kind household, your responses would be inclined to be kind to others, since this is what was modeled for you.

Part of the power of Now, though, is that our destinies are not predetermined by the historical data alone. We can retrain the model even if we came from difficult circumstances. So it is with AI. We can retrain it with new information and new insight and teach it to make better decisions.

In the conversation around ethical use of AI, this is where we must remember that we are the ones in control. We are the ones who determine the input. We are the ones who train the model, who set the boundaries. Neglecting to do so is reckless.

The difference between our brains and artificial intelligence comes down to two primary factors: our ability for split-second response between stimulus and response, and our free agency in decision-making.

For instance, think back to the earlier story of me going to the Wipro headquarters after I had already failed their assessment. There was a very low chance of success based on the data and context available. My own human will and intuition overrode these, which began my journey to where I am now.

Or when I chose to leave my PalmPilot in Karen's purse after our disastrous first date. This was a decision that contradicted the available information of the best course of action. Yet this one human decision led to the start of our relationship—not to mention the four lives that have come from my decision.

We are not subservient to an algorithm. Our great strength as humans is our ability to weave in emotion, intuition, spirituality, and ethics to allow us to override the programming. The analysis performed by the human brain goes beyond the data and situational context AI depends upon.

These strengths are irreplaceable. They are what makes us human and sets us apart from machines.

The benefit of artificial intelligence is in amplifying our human intelligence. We do not have to replace or replicate our strengths in order to minimize our weaknesses.

> The benefit of artificial intelligence is in amplifying our human intelligence. We do not have to replace or replicate our strengths in order to minimize our weaknesses.

To err is human, after all. This is where we need the most amplification. AI can help us *limit* human error, as we see occurring in automation. AI can help us create more insight, as we see in complex data analytics, so we have a fuller picture of what is true. In the past, we had only our intuition, which could be swayed by misinformed assumptions. By coupling the strength of our human intuition with AI-generated insights, we amplify our intelligence in decision-making. This makes us better humans.

Better Humans, Better Leaders

We shape our growing identity with each new Now, each new decision. The issue is not "humans or AI" but rather "humans *with* AI."

Since AI does not have the free agency or conscience of humans, the ethical responsibility falls to us as leaders. The human element is what will direct the course of AI. Artificial intelligence will amplify not only our intelligence but also our actions, for better or worse.

Doubtless you have heard much about the dangers of AI—stories of self-driving cars running into jaywalkers, stories of bias in AI recruitment tools, examples of racial stereotyping in AI-generated images, and so on. Yet these instances, when you dig deeper, expose the true culprit—us.

Like every innovation before it, AI bears the imprint of its creator. It can be used as a tool for good or a tool for evil. This comes down to our choices as leaders for how we will use AI. Will we make short-term decisions from a limited scope of selective data? Or will we be brave enough to grow our moral database and gain clarity of context?

I'm encouraged by how leaders like Sam Altman at OpenAI are setting up safeguards to protect children, or how AI is being used to report and remove exploitative material from the web. These examples highlight how, when leaders make ethical choices, technology can make the world a better place.

We must decide now what kind of future we want to create. What world do we want to leave to our children and grandchildren? To the generations we may never meet?

I, for one, think of this all the time. I think back to my grandmother—and the Now that led to her being taken in by my great-grandparents whom I never knew. I think about the universal ripple of good that came from this one kind act. It laid the foundation for my very identity today.

For there is yet another major difference between us and AI. We humans have a soul. We have a connection to one another that transcends time and technology. Together we form one Now.

I agree with what World Economic Forum (WEF) founder Klaus Schwab said on the topic: "In the end, it all comes down to people and values. We need to shape a future that works for all of us by putting people first and empowering them," and not allowing technology to "robotize" humanity.[8]

It is not enough to ask what AI can do for us in the present. We have a moral obligation, a spiritual imperative, to ask the hard question, "Will this do good for the world or harm?" If we choose

---

8   Klaus Schwab, "The Fourth Industrial Revolution: What It Means, How to Respond,"
WeForum.org, January 14, 2016, https://www.weforum.org/agenda/2016/01/
the-fourth-industrial-revolution-what-it-means-and-how-to-respond/.

good, then good will follow. If we choose limited self-interest, then we cannot be surprised when the universe repays in harm.

The principles of leadership—whether being applied to AI or to life—are no different. You start with the Why, move to the What, and then proceed with the How of any choice you are considering. The problem is, too many leaders try to start with How before they have a clear understanding of Why or What.

In this way, AI can also make us better leaders. It can help guide us to the true Why if we use it to create insight. It can amplify our intelligence in a way that has little to do with technology but every-thing to do with the mind and spirit. The question about how to use AI should help us pause, learn, analyze, and think before we act. It should compel us to define the Why and What. In this meditative process, AI can illuminate the dangers and risks before us. It can support or sway our intuition.

The question before us is whether we as leaders can demon-strate intellectual integrity and courage when faced with today's challenges. I won't pretend to know all the answers. I, too, am a learner on this journey.

By demystifying AI, we are forced to also demystify our own motivations as leaders. What kind of impact do we want to make on people? On the world? What does the database of our experiences and the context of the moment tell us? If life is indeed a series of Now, the time is now for us to decide what tomorrow will look like.

Leadership in the Age of AI

I tell senior executives, "You should have the least stress." ... Why? You're in charge. Why don't you delegate the stress? People don't dislike hard work. What people dislike is being out of control.

—JEFF BEZOS

One of my go-to phrases when someone asks how I'm doing is to answer, "Oh, I'm just leading the glamorous life of a tech CEO." The irony in this statement is thick, to say the least. When I became CEO, I like to say that I got much more funny and much more lonely overnight. Certainly, my position is a privileged life—I'd never argue otherwise. Every day, I am grateful for the trajectory of my career and the financial security it has brought to my family.

Yet the irony is that the life of a tech CEO appears far more glamorous on the outside than it is on the inside. To echo the sentiment of Jeff Bezos, yes, CEOs *should* be the least stressed. We have a whole team of people who report to us to carry out the work we wish to get done, after all.

Our stress levels are high, though, because we have the most consequential job. Every employee's well-being relies on the decisions made at the top to maintain a growing company. This is not the case with the lower ranks within a company. We often feel stressed because we are fixated on what we cannot control.

If you think back to COVID-19, consider how it affected our collective stress. The variables were high. In the early days, there were a lot of unknowns, so stress levels went through the roof. Once there were some guidelines, it gave people a sense of control and stress went down.

This can often be the day-to-day for a CEO. The more data we have on an issue, the better judgment we can show in decisions. More control means less stress. But when there is no information or context is lacking? There is little control but maximum stress.

Back in chapter 6, I mentioned that those of us in leadership positions in the present now must recognize that we are in a moment of management transition. The corporate culture we entered as young professionals is quickly becoming antiquated and being replaced by a new ethos of how the workplace should run.

Rather than waste time arguing about the pros and cons of this change or complaining about "the way things used to be," we can make far more progress if we approach the changing ethos with a positive curiosity. We have a long history as humans that proves the future is better than the past—much of it thanks to technology.

In some ways, I grapple with a sense of "imposter syndrome" when discussing leadership. With five years under my belt as CEO of a start-up, I pale in comparison to the CEOs I have admired for years. So rather than descend into a diatribe about what a leader should be or should not be, it would be better to simply discuss what I have *learned* in my time as CEO.

This chapter would look very different if I were to rewrite it five years from now, so nothing here is the "gospel truth"; it is just reflective of my own learning experience. Yet if something here resonates with you or provides you some comfort or insight, then I'm grateful to share it with you.

Modern leaders recognize that learning can come from anywhere. Remember the lesson I learned from the shoe shiner? Life is a great teacher if you keep your eyes open for lessons.

Parcells's Law

You are likely familiar with Murphy's law: "Anything that *can* go wrong *will* go wrong." One of my favorite expansions of this concept comes from Hall of Fame NFL coach Bill Parcells. When offering some advice to another coach—Mike Zimmer—he made the following three points, which I've slightly paraphrased:

First: Your best friends will disappoint you.

Second: Four or five things will happen every day that you wish wouldn't happen. If you can't handle those, then you need to get another job.

And third: It's lonely.

Otherwise, the rest of the job is fun.[9]

If you haven't figured it out already, all of these could also apply to executive leadership. While we intuitively understand that the people closest to us are the most likely to disappoint us, it still stings when it happens. And when it does, we have to recalibrate and remember the times we have disappointed others.

---

9   Ben Goessling, "Bill Parcells' Advice to Mike Zimmer," ESPN.com, January 19, 2014, https://www.espn.com/blog/nflnation/post/_/id/113678/bill-parcells-advice-to-mike-zimmer.

There are always consequences for such disappointment—some more severe than others—so I'm not advocating that we completely disregard when people let us down. But we should not be surprised by it. We should not let disappointment lead to more problems but rather approach the disappointment with empathy and a view for correction.

The day of the CEO is filled with the unexpected—especially at a tech start-up. The unexpected is our modus operandi—but more on this later. We can either complain about what goes wrong that we weren't expecting—or we can expect it. This may seem like a pessimistic view at first, but it has a very positive message.

Expecting things to go wrong keeps you on your toes, keeps you alert and agile. It keeps you focused on problem-solving. Plenty of jobs exist that are generally predictable and pay well. Executive leadership is not among them.

This is exactly what makes the position so lonely. Not everyone can understand the pressure you're under. Yes, you are often in the spotlight—but never forget that this is both a blessing and a curse. Like for the head coach of a football team, the ultimate responsibility of victory or loss falls at your feet. Yet there are many moving pieces out of your control.

Your star quarterback will get injured during the playoff game. The ref will call a penalty you don't agree with. It will start to rain buckets. Each of these can be a reason for stress to spike.

But they can also become opportunities. You can recalibrate. You can iterate. You can create morale.

The context for why Parcells was giving this advice should not be missed. He was offering this wisdom to Coach Zimmer as a way to support him. There is a great lesson here for learning to fight the loneliness of being a CEO. Seek out others who understand what you're going through.

When your day-to-day pursuits are about pushing yourself to the edge, it's natural to need to blow off steam. Some people do this through physical exercise—surfing, marathons, hundred-mile bike rides. These activities in and of themselves can be meditative. In my case, golf has been my go-to because I'm never competing against anyone but myself.

Community with other leaders is vital for fighting off loneliness. When I go out on the golf course, it's often with my peers—other tech CEOs and executive leaders who have a natural empathy for what I face. As we play a round, we discuss our lives, offer advice to one another, become sounding boards for ideas—or at the very least a listening ear when one of us simply needs to vent.

And speaking of coaches, I even got an executive coach for myself. Certainly, this can be a more expensive measure, but my coach has helped me grow into the leader I want to be. In the end, it's been the best investment I've made to better myself so I can show up as my best self for others.

My family has been another outlet for me. Spending time with them is a constant reminder of why I do what I do—especially on the difficult days. I've found experiencing the world through the natural wonderment of a child's eyes to be rejuvenating and therapeutic.

Whatever you do, do *not* sit in the loneliness. Find your release; find your community. Together, you can have more confidence to face the mountain before you.

Climbing the Mountain

Born in 1959, Ed Viesturs is a mountain-climbing legend. He is currently the only American who has climbed all fourteen of the world's highest mountains—that is, peaks over eight thousand meters. If that's not impressive enough, consider the fact that he's only the fifth person to ever accomplish this feat ... *without* using supplemental oxygen.

When he's not climbing, he is a motivational speaker. I met him while I was working at TIBCO and invited him to speak at our seminar, which was fittingly named "Scale Up." I asked him then if there was one particular quality necessary for someone to become a mountaineering legend.

He answered, "When you're climbing up a mountain, especially if you're doing it without oxygen, you take two steps—and then you have to literally stop for minutes to catch your breath. Then you take another two steps."

He went on to describe that at such high altitudes, it's not only the lack of oxygen affecting you—but the lack of water. You're always thirsty even though you're surrounded by ice. And nauseous to boot. As a result, sometimes you're going to slip back a step or two. Which means you have to take those steps all over again once you've caught your breath.

I couldn't ask for a more perfect analogy for life as an entrepreneur or as a CEO at a start-up. Building a start-up can feel like climbing a mountain in rarefied air. It's constantly two steps forward, catching your breath, and trying to push another two steps forward.

Not to mention that the consistent sliding back can quickly become discouraging. When this happens, you have to garner the courage and conviction to take two more steps. This is how courageous and successful companies are built and what sets them apart.

Lots of companies can take a step forward—even two. The real metric of success, however, is being able to string enough two-step segments together despite the setbacks. The story of many start-ups is one of valiant effort and hard work but never reaching the pinnacle. Sadly, these companies may create much of the innovation that helps others reach the peak, yet they are not credited or remembered.

One of the stories Ed shared with us was about the deadly expedition to Everest in 1996 that was later written about in the 1999 book

Into Thin Air, by Jon Krakauer. He was there at the exact same time and said they had planned to climb the mountain the same day. But when they looked at the clouds coming in, they decided to go back into their tent, because experience had taught them they wouldn't have enough time to get up and down safely.

They chose to be patient and wait. When the group hit by the storm came down, thousands of media people had gathered to document the event. Meanwhile, he and his partners scaled the mountain eleven days later, going up and coming down without incident. Despite their successful climb, was anyone waiting to take their picture or grab an interview? Of course not.

There's a lesson here for leaders—often when you do things the right way, no one will notice. Accolades do not automatically follow every successful choice you make. Human nature often fixates on the crashes, on the disasters. People will remember the one wrong decision but fail to notice the ten good ones.

Obviously, mountaineering is dangerous, uncomfortable work. "If you want to know how it feels to live on a mountain," Ed explained to me, "ask your best friend to come to your house, go into the cupboard with him—that's your sleeping arrangement for the next four months. Also, no plumbing. No water. No heat. Just eight layers of clothing in the cold."

Despite these difficulties, Ed and his team had essentially made mountaineering "boring" because they planned so well. As he put it, "For me, every trip had to be a return trip." While the outcomes are never guaranteed, the more predictable—or boring—you can make your work, the more likely you are to succeed. Create specific tenets of your decision-making process that you will not violate, come what may. Be courageously patient enough to wait out the storm in your tent. It could be the difference between life and death for your business.

There's a lesson here, too, about the role of AI in aiding a leader's decision-making. With more insight, more information, more context—you can gain more confidence about when to climb the peak and when to stay in the tent. You can never predict everything, but the more knowns you have within your view, the more likely you are to succeed.

Relevancy and recency also play a role here. The better the information available, the more likely you are to string two steps together and rebound from the occasional step backward. The success we've experienced at SingleStore has been evidence of this philosophy. Our team has had courageous patience and perseverance to keep stepping forward even when the oxygen was getting thin.

Courage is not a one-time action. It is a choice you make repeatedly, despite the difficulties. When you repeat an action, it becomes muscle memory. Repetition connects your memory, your context, and your choice into Now. It becomes a part of your identity, your culture, and directly leads to your outcomes—positive or negative.

Missionaries over Mercenaries

I've always prided myself on the people I've hired, but I came to a realization a few years ago. My deciding metric had often been relatability—which meant I was favorably disposed to people who reminded me of myself at that specific juncture of their career. Unfortunately for me, this is not a very reliable metric for whether someone will work out.

At first, I had no awareness I was doing this, but over time I've learned to adjust the criteria for whom I hire. Some of the best hires I've made at SingleStore are actually people who are the *least* like me.

As a leader, creating a healthy culture is one of your most important responsibilities. Creating culture falls into three categories:

1. What you promote. This is easy. This is the fun part of the job where you get to verbalize the mission, the vision, and the values.

2. What you practice. This is harder, because it means you have to back up what you are promoting. You have to live out the values you proclaimed—or else you're a hypocrite.

3. What you permit. This is the hardest. Here is where you have to set the boundaries of what you will allow—and what you won't.

The most difficult decision you will make as a CEO is when you fire the highest performer who continues to behave like a jerk despite repeated warnings. We all have such people in our companies. But if you prioritize the long-term health of the company and its culture, then there can be no excuse for bad behavior. In the end, it does much more damage than good, but the decision requires a lot of gumption.

The impact of each category works in reverse. That is, what you permit has the greatest impact where what you promote has the least. When people see what is allowed and not allowed, it shapes their decisions. And as HubSpot CEO Brian Halligan once said, "Culture is how people make decisions when you're not in the room."

Which is why you need to build a culture of missionaries over mercenaries. I picked up this particular idea through the writing of Nassim Taleb. In *Antifragile*, he presents a notion of how many of our companies are filled with mercenaries—people who are making massive wealth yet have nothing at stake.

On the flip side, missionaries live up to their name because they are driven by mission. They are willing to put everything on the line for what they believe.

Mark Zuckerberg showed himself to be a missionary when he declined Yahoo's $1 billion offer to buy Facebook. How many twenty-one-year-olds would turn down $1 billion? Not many.

Mercenaries care little about what they are fighting for and more about what they get out of it. Once they find a better offer elsewhere, they leave. This is counterproductive for a culture of innovation. The biggest companies in Silicon Valley have inadvertently led others to think that innovation happens when you give people unlimited food, gyms, and beanbag chairs. If anything, however, such perks end up leading to complacency and entitlement.

Meanwhile, missionaries are so dedicated to the mission, they innovate from frugality. This is the case time and again with lean start-ups—they live out the old proverb of "necessity is the mother of invention." They are the explorers who boldly go into the unknown and cultivate the wilderness.

If you want alignment in your company, then culture by definition is the greatest alignment you can create as a leader. It sets you up to make good decisions—for your team to make good decisions—so you can put two consecutive steps together, one after another.

Ultimately, missionaries are the ones who can take two steps forward after the step back. Mercenaries will pack up and abandon you on the mountainside when conditions get too harsh. The missionaries will stay beside you and help you up.

This has proven to be another way I've combated CEO loneliness—my executive team at SingleStore. Because they are willing to tackle many of the difficult decisions we encounter, it makes my load a little easier. We spend time together bonding over a meal or rolling up our sleeves at off-site meetings. In these contexts, we're able to develop a deep authenticity with one another.

When it comes down to it, always bet on a missionary over a mercenary.

We've all seen what happens when a sports franchise tries to build a team of superstars with headline-making salaries. With few exceptions—like the '90s Bulls led by Jordan—it almost always backfires. Compare this to teams who focus on players who are unified around a singular vision of victory.

If you can surround yourself with missionaries, then you'll build a great company. If you put mercenaries in charge, they'll always disappoint you.

Communication

Whole books have been written about the art of communication in leadership, but I'd be remiss to not mention it here. Simply put:

Communicate, communicate, and communicate some more.

I've learned there's no such thing as overcommunication in leadership. I can recall times when I thought I had overcommunicated, when I was afraid I would step into the realm of micromanagement. Yet time and again, the feedback I received was "We're not clear about this."

Communication is not always about the information. It largely depends on the context. Naturally, my team could not read my mind—they could not grasp the full context of my thinking. The responsibility fell on me to repeat with clarity and high frequency.

One of the leadership lessons I had to unlearn centered on how to handle vulnerability within communication. When I first took over as CEO, I thought it was my job to absorb all the bad news and only distill good news back to the team. I saw myself as a filter, a shield. But this is not how the team perceived it.

At first, I was frustrated by their response, which boiled down to "Management is cagey." I thought to myself, *Here I am, drinking the poison for them, and they're upset with me for not sharing the poison with them!*

Looking back, I can see that this was a well-intentioned but novice move on my part. I had to learn that it's actually good to share both the good *and* the bad news with the team. Doing so created the kind of transparency and trust they wanted out of me as a leader. And frankly, I was only hurting myself, stockpiling stress by keeping the bad news to myself plus the additional stress of the feedback.

It's a counterintuitive instinct to share bad news. As parents, we want to shield our kids from bad news. We want them to retain their innocence, their spark—and this is how I was thinking of our team.

But guess what? Your employees are not your kids. I had to accept that our organization was made up of tenacious adults who appreciated transparency around the reality of the situation. In fact, *appreciate* is too soft a word. For them, bad news was fuel for cultivating a problem-solving culture, to ask, "What can we do better? What can we do to help you?"

> As a leader, communicating bad news to your employees can be fuel for cultivating a problem-solving culture.

Lack of communication and lack of vulnerability are forms of self-isolation. You can combat CEO loneliness by inviting others in. By trusting them with more, they trust you with more. When you think about it, our relationships with each other are very karmic—you get what you give.

Into the Unknown

Perhaps the greatest challenge faced by CEOs is the amount of context switching demanded by the role. People underestimate this part of the job when they see it from the outside. Each hour of the average day is devoted to divergent issues. One hour you're in a product meeting, the next you're interviewing a candidate for a senior role, the next hour you're taking a customer to lunch, the next you're in a sales meeting, and so on.

It can feel like you're a juggler—but instead of only juggling balls, you're also juggling a handkerchief, a knife, a cup, a saw, and a Rubik's Cube. It can become overwhelming for anyone.

We have to constantly put everything in its proper context—and find a way to keep taking the next step. It's like the stonecutter analogy from Kobe Bryant. Every day, you keep swinging the hammer, knowing each swing layers the impact. Eventually, the stone will break. The steps will add up. What's unknown is how long this can take.

As I mentioned before, only a handful of people are comfortable with the unknown. To quote the poet William Blake (and also Doors front man Jim Morrison), "In the universe, there are things that are known, and things that are unknown, and in between, there are doors."

Meanwhile, being a CEO or a tech entrepreneur means spending 95 percent of your day dealing with the unknown. It takes a lot of bravery to open the door between the known and unknown. The risk averse will choose to stay put in the status quo.

Don't get me wrong—it's far more sane to stay in the known. We humans are trained by our brains to be happiest when an outcome is predictable. It's why rom-coms and Hallmark movies are so popular. When faced with the unexpected, most people don't know what to do. They have no information or context to draw on. They freeze up.

Leaders must be tenacious. They have to be able to recover quickly from a dejection, from stumbling. This is the hardest part, because it's easier to give up and climb back down rather than figure out how to take the next step forward.

The explorers, the visionaries, the innovators—they open the door between the known and unknown. This does not mean they have to do so blindly. Like the ancient navigators who looked to the stars to guide them through the unknown of the vast ocean, we can chart our course to discovery.

It is up to us to set our North Star—our Why, our mission—and to set the boundaries of how far we are willing to drift north, south, east, and west. It is our duty to keep up the morale of everyone on the ship. We cannot do this locked away in the captain's quarters. We have to be on deck, engaged and using every tool at our disposal to see ahead.

Like the spyglass or compass before it, artificial intelligence is such a tool. It does not set the destination. It does not steer the ship. But it can help illuminate the best course to bring information and context from the unknown into the known so you can make better choices.

Your greatest weakness and strength as a leader is the same—you are human. As a human, you will make mistakes. But also as a human, you have a great capacity for approaching every problem with creativity, compassion, and conviction.

Conviction is the hardest of these three. If you lack conviction, you can never be a good leader. You may be wrong or right, but you can never be confused in your decisions. Especially when it's not obvious to anyone else.

The courage of conviction is rarely backed up by data. When it is, it becomes obvious. It enters the realm of the known. When making decisions about the unknown, it is only in hindsight that it becomes obvious what the right choice was. The majority of your executive team may disagree with you—and if you're wrong, well, then it could cost you your company, your financial well-being, and your legacy. This thought causes me no small amount of nausea.

But if you can consistently connect the dots, find the pattern across a universe of dots to make conviction-based decisions, then you can keep putting one foot in front of the other.

Remember—there is no one "thing" that makes a company successful. The same can be said for leaders. No hack or trick up the sleeve will do it for you. It's a series of taking small, incremental steps, one after another, stacking good thoughts through decisions. Together, these create great companies. Together, these create great leaders.

CONCLUSION

In many ways, it's wrong to call this the "conclusion." While this may be the end of the book, it should be seen as the beginning of a conversation.

After all, the experience I've shared here is unique to me. It is *one* view—not the *only* view. When we add our views together, we create more insight. We collectively combine the pillars of Information, Context, and Choice to amplify each other's intelligence.

Whether you read this book from start to finish or jumped around to the topics of most interest to you, I hope my experience has helped demystify AI for you. I hope this has been a practical guide to give you more context on how to approach life, artificial intelligence, and leadership.

It is in these three areas that I want to leave you with a few final thoughts—again, not to end the conversation but to help transition into the next Now, the next discussion.

Life

If I have learned anything in my own journey, it is that life never moves in a straight line. Business is no different. It's about putting steps together in the right direction, putting yourself in a position to succeed repeatedly. In this context, failure is not always a setback but a part of the process.

Perhaps you're familiar with the law of wasted effort. For example, a lion succeeds in taking down prey in only one out of every seven attempts. Does it give up? Of course not. The entire animal kingdom is okay with successive failures. Only humans are frustrated by it and become discouraged.

Your pursuits become easier if you accept that you will never bat a thousand. In fact, you will increase your likelihood of success if you believe this.

Empirical evidence shows that we fail at least as much as we succeed. Those who put forth more effort naturally have a higher probability of success.

Along the way, you could meet someone who changes everything for you. For me, this was meeting Vivek and the subsequent move to the US with TIBCO. But had I not been putting forth the effort, I would have missed this chance.

Looking back, I can pinpoint five or six key events that had a phenomenal effect on my life—many of which I've included in this book. But you never know when those are going to happen. They cannot be forced or rushed. You must simply treat each day as a new adventure and head into uncharted territory. Enjoy it, and accelerate. That's what being alive is about.

Artificial Intelligence

As with many aspects of life, truth rarely rests at the extremes. It is usually in the middle. So it is with artificial intelligence. It is neither the savior of mankind nor the harbinger of our doom. It is not a magic silver bullet for future success. Nor will it pay for the sins of the past.

In approaching AI, it's helpful to look back at the history of gold rushes, especially the California Gold Rush of 1849. Only a small group of lucky individuals actually became rich off gold. The ones who attained more steady, assured success were those who *supplied* the miners—the clothing manufacturers making the boots and hats, the tools suppliers selling sieves and pickaxes. These were the ones who leveraged the gold rush for long-term profit.

AI is the latest gold rush. But will you be the one trying to pry it out of the ground—or will you be the one supplying the tools?

Either way, your success is rooted in getting your data in order. Do you have the right information available at the right time to create insights? At SingleStore, these are the questions we are helping organizations answer so they can know where to dig for gold rather than wandering aimlessly.

Leadership

In the last chapter, I spoke to the importance of patience in leadership. It bears repeating here. It's easy to succumb to false urgency, to rush to a decision. One of the ways I've grown as a leader is in how I've become a better decision maker over the past five years.

Even when a choice appears obvious, I sit on it for an extra day—or week, even. This ensures that I have all the proper information and context to make the right choice. Nor do I make a decision when I'm tired. When something comes up at the end of the day, I've learned to say, "I'll decide in the morning."

When decisions are less obvious, I use this "waiting period" to bounce ideas off my executive team and other confidants. Not only does this relieve the loneliness that comes along with decision-making; it allows me to invest trust in the team. It heightens the quality of the final choice because they can provide more information and context to create insight I could never generate on my own.

Courageous leadership does not mean you are never afraid. Rather, it's when you're the only person who *knows* you're afraid. As a leader, everyone is looking to you for their cues. If you are calm, they will be calm. If you are transparent, it robs much of fear's power over you.

In the age of AI, we leaders must remember that we have a moral responsibility to neither run from AI nor exploit it. We must set the boundaries of what we will promote, what we will practice, and what we will permit. Otherwise, we abandon control, conscience, and conviction.

Starting the Conversation

The explosion of artificial intelligence and its business implications feels like uncharted territory. In many ways, it is. The world is getting faster—but this has *always* been true. From the printing press democratizing information to me lugging a computer up flights of stairs to convince businesses they needed to modernize. From the steam-powered engine revolutionizing transportation to AI creating efficiency and insight.

No one person has all the answers. More conversations need to happen around these topics, for there is yet more insight to be created.

Think of it like *The Godfather*. The movie trailer gives you only enough information and context for you to decide to watch the movie. And even though the movie is three hours long, if you were to watch the deleted scenes, it would create more insight into the characters and plot. And if you then choose to read the source novel by Mario Puzo, you would find even more information and context.

So it is with this book. Consider this the movie trailer. There is more to be explored in how we leaders can use AI for good. And not only for good in business but for good in the world.

We may find areas where we agree—and areas where we disagree. So long as the conversation is respectful, I'm a firm believer that we can all learn from one another.

Let's take this conversation off the pages of this book, then, and into Real Time with one another. If you've enjoyed the insights here, I invite you to engage with me through LinkedIn:

Or with our team at SingleStore:

An eternity lives in Now. The time for this conversation is Now. Do not put it off for tomorrow. There is no time like the present. It truly is a gift.

For Now sits at the crux of Information, Context, and Choice. Now is the time for courageous leadership. Now is the time for creating insight. Now is the time to put one foot in front of the other and move forward. Now is all we have ... because time **is** Now.

APPENDIX

A Conversation with

Vinod Khosla

If you made it this far, then you've come with me on the journey of demys-
tifying AI, how we got to today, and what we are seeing just around the
corner. I wanted to leave you with this—a glimpse into what the future
will be with one of the most insightful, successful, and intelligent people I
have the opportunity to know, Vinod Khosla.
Read on to see what the future may be.

· ·

RAJ: Allow me to let you in on a conversation between me and Vinod
Khosla, founder of Khosla Ventures. Vinod focuses on investing
in bold technology ideas that can disrupt massive industries. He
was previously a cofounder of DayZ Systems and founding CEO
of Sun Microsystems, where he pioneered open systems and com-
mercial risk processes.

Vinod is not just a successful entrepreneur and investor. At his
core, he is a mentor and an advisor. Driven by a desire to create
positive change through technology, he has a passion for empowering entrepreneurs and believes business can be a force for good.

Vinod, you and I have spoken about when I was growing up in India and studying computer science, how you were always an inspiration for all of us. You had started a company that we all looked up to and I later worked for, which was Sun Microsystems. Tell us a little bit about your early life and leading up to Sun and the idea around Sun.

. . . .

VINOD: One thing that's always intrigued me is starting a company. A long, long time ago, I read the story of Intel starting up and of Andy Grove, a Hungarian immigrant, starting that company in Silicon Valley. That caught fire in my imagination and convinced me to go start a company.

As soon as I was done with college, I actually jumped into wanting to do a start-up. I came to Silicon Valley and did my first start-up, which is a CAD tools company called DayZ Systems. It was quite successful, went IPO, and did very well for the three of us who started it. What I realized was that there was no computing platform on which one could develop applications like DayZ.

So we spent more money developing our platform on which to build the CAD application—and I was an electrical engineer—than we spent on the application itself, and that's what got me to think about starting the platform company. I looked around, saw the technology at Stanford—"sun" actually stands for Stanford University Net—which was where the name came from. And so that was pretty exciting, and the rest is history.

. . . .

RAJ: One thing that I've always found in our conversations is that, for you, *impossible* is just an opinion. And I think you made a lot of things that seemed impossible absolutely not only possible but part of everyday life.

I've always admired your vision, or your ability to see around corners into the future, some would say. I think it was almost ten or twelve years ago when you wrote an article that said that doctors are going to be a thing of the past. Just to be a little provocative, what are your predictions about the next ten or twenty years?

. . . .

VINOD: One of the things about technology that has always excited me was how much transformation it can drive. When I started Sun, the microprocessor was just coming on the scene. It sounded silly to me, that Digital Equipment Corporation, DEC, a company most people don't remember but that was the dominant computer company—maybe the number two computer company in the world after IBM—had to take a processor with roughly the same power and share it among lots and lots of users when it cost one hundred dollars for a microprocessor. That idea led to Sun.

And while that idea led to Sun, it also led to the idea of TCP/IP. So Sun adopted TCP/IP in 1982. And I've seen these transformations go on from time to time.

When I said in 1982, if you had a desk at Sun, you were required to have email. None of those pink slips for messages that were the standard of the day—and that was 1982. People laughed when in 1985 I said that Grandma will one day use email on a PC.

When 1995 came along, we bet on TCP/IP as an exponential growth technology when every major telco I talked to said two things—I actually remember AT&T telling me that nobody needs more than ISDN at home, 64 kilobits. And that TCP/IP is too flaky a system. So, in 1996 we started Juniper Networks.

This type of large technology transformation has always gone on, and what it takes is some sort of driver, usually an instigator—an individual who causes all that change to happen. I've seen these large transformations brought around by technology, and literally nobody believed TCP/IP was important in 1996 when we started Juniper, which was a natural successor to Sun. As you remember, Sun used to say, "The network is the computer." We needed a networking tool like TCP/IP, and Juniper was a 500 times return on a $3 million initial investment, which is about $7 billion in return. That was back in the '90s. I have followed these trends constantly.

We can talk about trends in any dimension, and there's infinite dimensions to go to.

It was in 2012 that I first wrote two blogs. One was called "Do We Need Doctors?" And the second was called "Do We Need Teachers?" To be fair, I imagined humans doing the human elements of medical care and education, which is probably 10 to 20 percent of what they do today. I didn't want to eliminate them. In fact, my big paper was then called "20 Percent Doctor Included" for the human element of care.

The idea that a physician can keep up with the latest five thousand articles on breast cancer when they're treating a breast cancer patient, doing research study, is preposterous. We have too much information for humans to keep in their head. And when you start connecting things like cancer, patients with cardiac disease, with other diseases, it gets extremely complex.

So I've always imagined that complexity will be handled by computers, and five years ago, when it was not very hot, we invested in OpenAI.

It's been exciting to see the vision of doctors and teachers come together. My wife runs CK-12 Foundation, a nonprofit that's doing AI tutoring for every kid on the planet, and I believe they can be nearly free. My son's working on an AI primary care doctor, which I'm very, very excited about. But we also have companies working on cardiologists, physical therapists, and all manner of human expertise that's within the AI domain.

There are so many other domains in which technology can make a difference. I'm quite convinced we can cost-effectively embrace every coal and natural gas plant in this country well before 2050 using fusion, and so we are working on fusion. I think we can replace the majority of cars in most cities with a very different notion of public transit, radically reinvented, where it's always faster than cars, always on demand, not on a schedule. And it can get from anywhere to anywhere at a very cost-effective price. No matter where I look, that's possible.

I think the sources of food, plant proteins, will change radically over the next twenty-five years. AI-based intelligence will see probably a billion bipedal robots within the next twenty-five years. Music and entertainment will be reinvented. Climate is, of course, a big issue—lots of work to do there. I could go on and on.

. . . .

RAJ: Do you think in our lifetime or in the next couple of decades you would see the "20 percent developer" emerge, taking from your 20 percent doctrine?

. . . .

VINOD: Almost certainly it'll happen. The way I would think about the software developer is that everybody below the median developer will be eliminated and a higher number will become natural language programmers, which we are starting to see. Below that, you shouldn't need to write SQL. You should explain what you want, and the system will write the SQL and access the database. The great developers will become excellent developers, and the 10x developers will be way more powerful than they are today.

You will need developers to architect systems and the 10x developers to visualize highly complex systems. So I do think they'll have a large, hugely amplified role. My bet is, the top 10 percent of developers will do more work than 100 percent of developers today.

. . . .

RAJ: I'm a father of four children, and two of my older kids are pursuing STEM-related studies at UC Berkeley. Do you think education in computer programming is still something you would encourage youth to pursue? Or are there other domains you would encourage them to seek?

. . . .

VINOD: Let me suggest the following. The need to work in human society will virtually disappear. People will work because they want to work on what they want to work on, not because they need to work to earn an income. So, suddenly, even being an artist will become a better job because people are doing it as their passion.

Having said that, I often get asked about how people should train for this world. And I think the most important thing is to develop the mind properly for young people. And I do think computer science, engineering, and STEM in general develops the mind in ways that are going to be generally more useful. My advice today is, don't become a specialist in one narrow area. Get as broad an education as possible, at least at the undergraduate level. Then if you want a PhD in electrical engineering or biotechnology, fine. Try to do something broad so you can pivot into a number of different areas.

As you know, the whole notion of chips and software at this scale didn't exist when I went to college in 1971, but because of my broad training—a master's degree in biomedical engineering after a degree in electrical engineering and an MBA—I was able to move as the world of technology moved, and I was able to pursue my passion for technology with more and more impact.

I talked about how Sun started. It was very, very tactical. It was nothing super strategic. But over time. I've realized the power of technology to make a huge positive difference on humankind, whether it is on energy production, fusion, or better, sustainable aviation fuel, or even food sources.

So, I would say get a broad education and keep learning. Learn enough to keep learning new areas. And develop a certain style of thinking in your brain, and you will be able to respond as the world changes, and it will change.

. . . .

RAJ: Getting on to the topic of entrepreneurship, you've been one yourself, and also partnered with legendary entrepreneurs. And one of the reasons I became an entrepreneur was because of you. What do you think are the key attributes or characteristics that make a successful entrepreneur?

VINOD: In my opinion, entrepreneurs generally are optimistic. Skeptics never did the impossible. You can give a hundred reasons Elon Musk couldn't be successful at starting a car company, let alone an EV car company, which practically didn't exist back then.

Entrepreneurs also have very rapid learning rates. They get in the field, they engage, and they rapidly iterate and adjust what they're doing. They have a passion for their vision but yet seek lots of input and are willing to adjust their vision as input comes in. It's an unusual combination. Really good entrepreneurs are very obstinate about their vision and very flexible about their tactics. They also build awesome teams, and they're not afraid to hire strong teams. You look for those characteristics in entrepreneurs.

RAJ: One piece of advice that you gave me was to be like a Formula One driver. If you go too fast, you'll crash; if you go too slow, you'll lose the race—and that's something I grapple with almost on a daily basis.

Your take on innovation has always been intriguing to me. You tell the story about one of the companies you were on the board of that raised some money, and you said something like "Let's raise an extra $50 million, as long as you are ready to 'waste' a little."

Can you talk about entrepreneurs and innovation, their almost addiction to innovation, and how that has changed the trajectory of companies?

VINOD: People don't like failing, and I like to say that my willingness to fail is what causes me to succeed. The big difference is, unless you try risky things, you're not going to do things differently than everybody else.

The market is very competitive. Hence, one area in which you can differentiate is to take larger risks for larger changes and larger innovation. Now, the key to that is, if you fail, you don't want to lose your company, so you want to take risks that might set you back a little bit. If they succeed, they double the market value or market opportunity of your company.

So asymmetric risks are what matters, very much in the Nassim Taleb sense—he's written on this topic [as author of books such as *The Black Swan* or *Antifragile*]. I always say, if you took half a percent or 1 percent of your market cap—and that applies to a five-person company and a five-thousand-person company and a fifty-thousand-person company—if you take half a percent of your market cap and put it on ten projects, every time you lose, you lose half a percent of your market cap; but if you win, you double your market cap.

I'll give you a classic example: Square's Square Cash. Square Cash was one of these experiments, and it is now the dominant part of what I think is perceived as the company's market cap. So, I like to say that failure doesn't count if it's an intelligent failure and the right size of failure.

I'm very excited by this notion that you can encourage people to try things that might fail and may even be likely to fail. But if you try enough of them, you have 5 percent downside in this formula and 500 percent upside.

RAJ: This has been a very valuable lesson for me personally and here at SingleStore. I think our model success is greatly attributable to the rate of innovation and our addiction to that.

Naturally, the topic of AI is extremely hot right now. You saw around corners there. I believe you're one of the largest investors in OpenAI. What was your first experience when you started hearing about or spoke to OpenAI, the vision and what got you to back them, and where do you see OpenAI and AI at large going in the next few years or the next decade?

VINOD: The thing one has to do is bet on something when others aren't betting on it.

We've seen hot trends, and everybody's doing the same thing, and then you get bubbled. We've seen that repeatedly over the last four years I've been dealing with innovation. You have to decide what is important, what will have a large impact and sustain through ups and downs. It was clear to me that it was likely, although not guaranteed, that AI would have a huge impact.

It was about five years ago when we invested in OpenAI and about ten years ago when I'd written and thought about whether we need doctors' expertise, whether we need teachers to teach students, and all kinds of other things from robotics—which is really dependent on AI intelligence.

So we placed the bet. In fact, we placed the largest bet I've ever placed in the forty years I've been in venture capital by a factor of two, and that has worked out very well. It started with this belief that AI was going to be important when there was no real hot trend and it wasn't an area where every corporation or investor had to be. Those are the right kinds of bets to place.

I think AI is going to affect all aspects of our life, but what I would say in an encouraging way is that we're not done with AI. We are less than 10 percent of the journey toward AGI. My personal belief is that large language models will be very, very important but not the only AI technique. We are spending time on what might look like a large language model four years from now. For example, we've invested in symbolic logic, probabilistic programming techniques to achieve the kinds of Bayesian thinking human beings do.

I look at human intelligence and types of human intelligence from creativity to logic and reasoning to others. It's very likely some of these things would emerge in large language models as emergent behavior of those models, but it's also very likely there'll be other add-ons to help AI become more versatile, broader, and eliminate most of the criticism you see today.

Your skeptics point to what's wrong with AI today. I always tell our team, "Look two years out, and most of the problems you're dealing with will be much, much smaller." Whether it's hallucination or the occasional logical or reasoning error. Five years ago, nobody imagined LLMs could write code. I think that capability will be significantly enhanced or get much better over the next five years. We are far from done.

In the future, I don't think people will ever do an API integration. They'll just tell the AI to do an integration for them. And APIs may still be needed, but the English language will be the way you do an integration—just tell it to integrate. And if it needs clarity, it'll ask you those questions.

I would venture to guess that half of IT departments fifteen years from now will be gone. I point to the following fact: in the 1920s, most corporations in the US had a VP of electricity; those roles are gone. I'm not suggesting the CIO will be gone, but half of the IT function, the very common function of BI or business intelligence, will be.

You have a business user who specifies something that they want done. The data analyst then turns it into SQL and into a query. The business analyst should be able to say, "Hey, do this report for me." They could go beyond that and say, "In the last three months, or in last quarter's data, what should I be looking at? What's an anomaly?" They don't even know the question they should be asking in the report, and AI should be able to answer a question without IT people involved. I do think we're going to see a very different world coming up that has much more capability and far fewer IT people. You'll still need the 20 percent, hugely amplified by AI. It's all very exciting.

. . . .

RAJ: What advice do you have for leaders, in tech or otherwise? In this fast-evolving field of AI, do you think the ocean of leadership and organizations and organization structure will change dramatically over the next decade or so, and if so, what are some of the things you should look out for to be successful?

. . . .

VINOD: A decade is a short time in which to see some of these changes. Some of the things I'm talking about, such as how you handle business processes in your company, will change well within the next ten years. You won't need a UiPath or Automation Anywhere or those kinds of clunky old systems. I think you'll still need great data architecture in a company.

From a leadership point of view, what has worked for the last ten years or twenty years or thirty years will probably not work. Whether it's in marketing or product design, the kinds of people you have is ambiguous as to what you will need. Leadership will be about putting a much more dynamic thinking organization in place, stretching their thinking, and having them look at what might come from left field to affect your business.

In five years for incumbents, their existing customers will be a huge advantage in making a transformation; leaders will need to be the consultant that brings all the latest approaches to them. That's the recipe for growth. The recipe that says, "I have my customers locked in and I can be insulated," won't work very well.

. . . .

RAJ: You told me a story about how you use AI a lot more than most common people do, and that you wrote a song for your daughter's wedding. How did that go?

. . . .

VINOD: I'm probably in the bottom first percentile of people when it comes to music capability. My daughter's wedding was in May, and I wrote the speech I was going to give as father of the bride. But then I told ChatGPT to turn that speech, that emotion I wanted to express, into a rap song. It did the lyrics. I then entered the lyrics into a new AI called Splash.ai that did the whole rapping—the instrumentals, the voice, the singing, the whole bit. So, I was able to play a very, very personal message in a rap song, a capability I couldn't even remotely have imagined. That's a great example—I didn't have that capability; now I do. People loved it. The quality was really high. I'd recommend that everybody try this.

RAJ: The stage is yours for any concluding remarks.

VINOD: I think, because of the exponential rate of growth in technology, the next ten years will see more change than we've seen in the last twenty-five years. If you want to look at how different 2033 will be from today in 2023, you have to go back into the 1990s and compare how different today is from the 1990s. The implication is that leaders will have to be much more dynamic in their thinking and in their organization.

My bet is that future IT systems, future organizations, future company configurations, will be optimized for change—not optimized for a particular function.

I find that most people are more limited by what they think they can do versus what they can actually do. My hope is that they can imagine the possible and then try to make that happen with technology.

It's a wonderful way to live.

ACKNOWLEDGEMENTS

First and foremost, I would like to extend my heartfelt thanks to Madhukar Kumar, Marcie Montague, and Adee Feiner, whose honesty, advice, and insights about what to cut—sparing no feelings!—made a big impact on the story. I am deeply indebted to you for your guidance, listening ears, and enthusiasm for this project.

A number of AI concepts in the book were inspired by my conversations with Madhukar as we were figuring out the company strategy in the world of generative AI and vector databases. It was these early conversations that led me to build out the framework that has become a key construct of demystifying AI for leaders.

To my dear parents, whose love and support have been the bedrock of my life, I express my profound gratitude. So many of the principles that blossomed in my life were planted by you.

To my wife, Karen, you have been by my side in this adventure called life as the most ardent and loyal supporter of my various pursuits. Your patience is infinite, for which I am grateful. Your laughter makes me happy, and your company makes me feel like the luckiest man in the world. This journey we are on would not have been possible or even worth it if you weren't in my life.

To our children, of all the things I am grateful for, and for all my achievements, none will ever come close to the privilege of being your dad. As they say in certain civilizations, the child chooses who their parent will be—thanks for choosing me to be yours. Your brilliance, creativity and curiosity remind me daily of the importance of leaving this world a better place than I found it. You are my inspiration, and why I am excited about what the future holds for humanity.

And to my friends—you know who you are. You've motivated, grounded, entertained, and inspired me, whether on the golf course, over a nice glass of Bordeaux, or cheering on our Golden State Warriors. Your friendship and support have helped me maintain my eternal optimism even in the face of challenges.

I am truly blessed to have such a remarkable network of friends, family, colleagues, and mentors in my life. Thank you all for being a part of this incredible journey.

ABOUT THE AUTHOR

Raj Verma's professional journey has spanned more than two decades in infrastructure software, from his formative years at PTC, to TIBCO, where he headed marketing, became chief revenue officer, and ultimately became COO. Raj then served as COO at Hortonworks and Apttus before becoming CEO at SingleStore in 2019.

As CEO of SingleStore, Raj has driven a seven-fold increase in revenues, raised more than $300 million and led the company's successful transition to the cloud, while continuously increasing the strength of the employee base four-fold.

While Raj is an avid golfer, reader, and pursuer of holistic health of mind, body, and spirit, he identifies first and foremost as a husband and father. He is married to the love of his life, Karen, and they are blessed with four amazing children. His philanthropic interests center around helping the vulnerable in our society, including the education of underprivileged children and addressing mental health issues of teenage women.

Raj earned his bachelor's degree in computer science from BMS College of Engineering in Bangalore, India, and he resides in California's Bay Area with his family.

CONTACT

For further insight into how data continually plays a pivotal role in AI, and how businesses are leveraging their data to enhance capabilities in both new and existing use cases, visit rajverma.com. Raj is a renowned speaker on the subjects of AI and real-time data. You have the opportunity to book Raj as a speaker through the website, where you can also find a wealth of resources and tools designed to assist your company in developing and implementing effective data strategies for AI.